In Search of

THE HIDDEN TREASURE
"The Pearl of Great Worth"

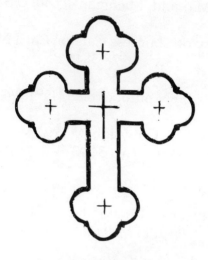

George Rapanos

B.S. (Pharmacy)
M.A. (Religious Studies)

Avensblume Press
1815 S. Saginaw Road
Midland, MI 48640

Published by Avensblume Press,
1815 South Saginaw Road,
Midland, Michigan 48640, U.S.A.

"Library of Congress Catalog Card Number:"
92-75844

ISBN number 0-9634591-0-4

Publisher's Cataloging in Publication
(Prepared by Quality Books Inc.)

Rapanos, George
 In search of the hidden treasure : the pearl of great worth /
George Rapanos.
 p. cm.
 Includes bibliographical references and index.
 ISBN 0-9634591-0-4

 1. Rapanos, George. 2. Spiritual life. 3. Myth in literature.
I. Title.

BL624.R35 1992   291.4
                                  QBI92-20216

This book is dedicated to the memory of my
father and mother.

Alexandros Nicolaous Rapanos

1899 - 1988

Nicoletta (Agnostopoulos) Rapanos

1908 - 1990

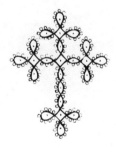

Who is to say what is real and what is not real . . .

The strangest things are true and the truest things are strange.

One should not be obsessed with a passing love or with the objects of this world. One should be in love with the beloved and the beloved is God. This Avens flower is only a flower but in its transcendental form it is the image and shadow of God.

CONTENTS

Dedication 1

Contents 5

Introduction 11

The Hidden Treasure 15
The Presence of God 16
Wrecked by Success 19
The Experience of Meditation 29
Faith Healing 30
Visualizing an Aura 32
Illusion 33
Annihilation 33
Various Forms of God-Consciousness 34
A Cosmic Vision 36
Love Your Enemy 37
Transcendence of Good and Evil 39
The Grace of God 40
Love of Self 49
Projection—The Enemy Within 51
Continuing the Journey 54
Purging 57
Beatific Vision 61
Finite to Infinite Consciousness 65
Continuing the Search 66
Validation 67

Poetry 71
George Rapanos
The Paradox 72
Immortality 73
The Angel and the Peacock 74

Intertwined 75
Spirituality 76
Rebirth 77
Revelation 78
Light and Beauty 79
The Hidden Treasure 80
A Heart Full of Love 81
Beyond the Horizon 82
The Pilgrim's Journey 83
Seeking God 84
A Gift from God 85
A Precious Gift 85
A Phantom of Delight 86
Rose from Above 86
Pilgrim's Quest 87

Ruth E Rapanos
Unseen Horizons 97
Life 97

Favorite Poems 99
Olive Branch 100
To Althea from Prison (excerpt) 101
The Daffodils 101
Ad Finem 102
A Psalm of Life 104
Sonnet 116 106
Sonnet 29 106
New Friends and Old Friends 107
The Day is Done 108
Thanatopsis 110
How the Great Guest Came 113
The Rhodora 115
Renascence 116
Hamlet (excerpt) 123
Hamlet (excerpt) 124

The Conference of the Birds (excerpt)   125
Memory   126
A Vanishing Friend   128
The Touch of the Master's Hand   129
The King Who Built a Splendid Palace   131
Winds of Fate   132
The Prayer of the Cock   133
The Fool's Prayer   134
A Drunkard Accuses a Drunkard   136
When I Was One and Twenty   137
The Devout Slave   138
The Devil Complains   138
Abou Ben Adhem   139
Annabel Lee   140
To My Old Yellow Dog   142
Annie and Willie's Prayer   144
Let the Lower Lights Be Burning   148
Prayers   149

A Hidden Treasure Myth   151

Favorite Wisdom Tales   159
Chinese Pilot   160
Footprints   169
The Value of a Gem   170
Unconditional Love   171
The Gates to Heaven and Hell   172
The Best of Two Potatoes   173
Publishing the Three Sutras   174
There Are Too Many Saviors On MY Cross   175
The Greatest Swordsmith   177
A Pile of Manure   178
Serenity   179
This, Too, Will Pass   180
A Matter of Projection   181
The Source of Eternal Life   182

Fear   183
Greed or Sorrow?   184
The Miser and the Angel of Death   185
Unity   186
An Unutterable Source of Existence   187
The Juggler of Notre Dame   188
Is That So?   192
Reality   193
Conditioning   194
The Gardner   195
Freedom   196
Awareness   198
I Want Your Finger   199
Weasel and the Well   200
God! Why Has Thou Forsaken Me?   207
Imitation   208
Death Speaks   209
Cause and Effect   210
Calling Card   211
Does the End Justify the Means?   212
Salvation   213
The Angel of Death   214
Acceptance   216
Ignorance   216
Enlightenment   217
Intuitive Perception   218
A Fable of Two Brothers   219
The Guarantor   231

Notes   233

Illustrations   1, 3, 4, 9, 13, 71, 74, 96, 99, 100, 125, 133,
                    141, 151, 159, 168, 172, 178, 180, 186,
                    195, 230, 232

THE HIDDEN TREASURE
"The Pearl of Great Worth"

There is a hidden Treasure,
Most search for it in vain.
It comes down from heaven,
And it falls like the rain.

This treasure is not one of silver,
This treasure is not one of gold.
The source of this hidden treasure,
Lies deep within one's soul.

A treasure more precious than silver,
A treasure more precious than gold.
To find this hidden treasure,
You must look within your soul.[14]

INTRODUCTION

In Search of The Hidden Treasure, "The Pearl of Great Worth," is a book dealing with religious transformation. It is an aggregate of various sources, filled with quotations, parables, poetry and wisdom tales as diverse as Buddha, Meister Eckhart, Edna St. Vincent Millay, Samuel Taylor Coleridge, Walt Whitman, and the Bible.

This book is both a spiritual autobiographical affirmation of my faith and encouragement to those who wish to follow the path that may lead them to spiritual fulfillment. It evolved from a religious revelation which I had in 1984, and it is an anguished, forthright attempt to come to grips with the religious issues which I found hostile and unfriendly and contained in daily life.

It is not as much the intent of this book to reveal a set of truths about God, as it is an attempt to convey, through its prose, poetry, quotations, parables, wisdom tales, and my own mythological story and poetic works, the intuition of reality that touches the heart, and burns and stirs the soul.

I have written what I feel is crucial and important in describing the reality of Truth, and to some extent the mystical events that took place in my life that made me aware of God's incomprehensible love, grace, virtue, and power.

It is only with the heart that one can see cleary:
What is essentaial is invisible to the eye.

In Search of
THE HIDDEN TREASURE
"The Pearl of Great Worth"

My search for Truth has taken me from a state of finite consciousness and conditional love, to the awareness of infinite consciousness of unconditional love.

After fifty years of living I became aware of the meaning and purpose of life. My hope is that those reading this book will become aware of this much sooner than I, so they may grow in spiritual consciousness to enjoy the splendor and spontaneity of the moment.

My dear friends,
With your kind permission, let me share it with you.

God's eternal love was bestowed on me by a transcendental and redemptive experience. The effect of this redemption has allowed me to accept God's incomprehensible love, grace, virtue, and power. God's grace transformed my heart, altered my nature, and changed the course of my destiny.

This change of heart, brought about through my suffering, made me aware of my own shortcomings. Redemption now fills me with love, compassion, and wisdom to understand man's suffering and accept the faults and transgressions of others.

The effect of man's suffering, if overcome, will produce a personal depth of conviction and an awareness of God's Being. In this joy all suffering will be transcended.

The love which now consumes me is no longer simply the love for the objects of the world or the love of man for God, but the love of God for all mankind. The ultimate in wisdom is to become aware of God's presence in the soul and act as an agent in fulfilling His will.

15

The Presence of God

The presence of God came upon me one afternoon when I was at the lake trying to start the motor on my boat. I tried for over an hour to start the motor without any success. A short distance away, people were gathering around a small boy who had fallen into the water. The boy had been brought out of the water unconscious and was not breathing.

There were two men attempting to revive him. I felt that their methods would fail so I pushed them aside and attempted to revive the boy by giving him mouth-to-mouth resuscitation. I knew I had only about four or five minutes before brain damage would occur. The boy remained motionless and started to turn purple when a terrible thought flashed through my mind. Because I believed I could do better, I would now be responsible for this boy's life or death.

This was an awful feeling of helplessness. I frantically applied heart massage along with mouth-to-mouth resuscitation. When I was beginning to think my efforts were in vain, he suddenly began to breathe. I continued mouth-to-mouth resuscitation until his color came back. I cannot adequately express in words how I felt and how relieved I was at that moment.

After the ambulance came and took the boy away, I went back and tried to start the motor on my boat again. My father-in-law had just arrived and said that it was God's will that had prevented me from starting the motor, so I would be there to save this boy's life. My remark was, "Nonsense! If that were the case then I would now be able to start the motor."

That is when I became conscious of something that made me aware that if I were able to start the boat at that time, I would rationalize and believe it was a coincidence rather than the hand of an unseen supernatural power that most call God. This Presence expressed to me, not with words, but through an awareness that it would show me in such a way that even I would believe in its existence.

I again attempted to start the motor. I kept trying for over an hour and finally conceded that there was no way in disproving this theory of a divine intervention, and that this supernatural awareness was only a figment of my imagination. The motor defiantly was not going to start. So I went home and completely forgot about this Presence. The magnitude of this rescue only inflated my ego. I thought I alone had saved that boy's life!

Many are called but few are chosen.

A week later, I was at the cottage waiting for my wife. She was to arrive at noon with the food and our two children. She was pregnant at the time. I waited and waited and finally called home to see if she had left. There was no answer. I began to worry as the time passed. Then a call came from the emergency room at the hospital.

I was told that my wife had had a very serious car accident. Suddenly, at that moment the mystical Presence again became very real and reassured me that everything would be all right. When I arrived at the hospital and saw that my wife was not injured, I quickly rushed into the emergency room. I saw my daughter lying on a table quite agitated, staring at the curtain separating her from her brother. I immediately pulled the curtain back so she could see him. When they smiled at each other, I knew they would be fine. My only concern now was for the welfare of our unborn child.

My wife told me that she had gone off the road and when she tried to get the Volkswagen back onto the highway, it had rolled over and over and caught fire. She found our daughter under the car and, while the car was in flames, she had reached under and pulled her away from the fire to safety. She then found our son, who was thrown by the force of the accident, a short distance from the car.

Later, I went and saw the car which had been consumed by the fire. It was a miracle that my family had survived, and this miracle was the supreme effect of God's grace. A miracle of divine intervention. A few days later, my wife had our baby, and she and the baby were fine.

I was not prepared at that time to acknowledge this gift of serendipity or accept this Presence into my heart and receive its gift of salvation. Salvation is the awareness and acceptance of His grace and presence within one's heart here and now.

> To those who are called according to His purpose, He will glorify.

Again, I forgot about this Presence and continued in life thinking that I was in control. I chose to ignore the Power within me that had my best interests at heart.

> Few of us choose to listen to the call. The call of grace in its ultimate form is a summons to be one with God.

Again I pursued that which I thought would bring me fulfillment. I had never believed in God as many people do—that anthropomorphic being that rules over all existence. At times I would expound my philosophy contrary to those who would insist that God truly existed.

> Alone, alone, all, all alone,
> Alone on a wide, wide sea!
> And never a saint took pity on
> My soul in agony.[2]

Wrecked by Success

My life was full of accomplishments, and I was very proud of them. I had a devoted wife and a beloved mother for my five wonderful children. I had a good education. I had many talents that afforded me many pleasures and a successful business that afforded me many luxuries. I was admired by many and respected by my alma mater for my contributions, as well as in my community, where I served in organizations that helped less fortunate people than myself.

I was in control. This is what I thought, because my life was going so well at the time. But what was driving me? I was more concerned with my success as a businessman than with the happiness and growth of my soul.

> For what does it profit a man to gain the whole world and forfeit his soul?
>
> Mark 8:36

I would periodically go to the doctor whenever I felt depressed. I thought that there was something physically wrong with me. I was always told that I was in excellent health, and that I should slow down.

> This somber glow I feel within me burning,
> Shall I, wretch that I am, confess it for love's yearning?
> Ah, no, it is salvation that I crave,
> Might such an angel come my soul to save!
>
> The Flying Dutchman

I had many problems with my family that caused me anxieties and emotional stress. I attempted to please them but no matter how hard I tried, there was always something that I did or did not do that dissatisfied them.

This I took as complete rejection, even to the point that it nullified all the good that I did. At that time in my life I was more concerned about what other people thought of me than what I thought of myself.

> Do not think that I have come to bring peace to the world. No, I did not come to bring peace, but a sword.
>
> I came to set sons against their fathers, daughters against their mothers, daughters-in-law against their mothers-in-law;
>
> A man's worst enemies will be the members of his own family.

Matthew 10:34-36

I believe that it was this suffering that motivated me to seek that which would bring me peace. And because of this suffering I came to a truth. I was affected as a child by my parents' lack of understanding, and their lack of unconditional love. For love is a state of being in which the satisfaction of the loved one is as important and desirable as that of the lover. Unconditional love accepts the faults of others, irrespective of the feelings, motives, and actions of the object of one's love.

My parents made judgments and observations without justification, because of their lack of awareness of my true nature and integrity. I resented it deeply, but was unaware that this form of incorrect perception and misunderstanding was to influence my future behavior at a very young age.

This desperate desire and need as a child for my parents' unconditional approval was being projected onto others. The hurt is diminished when you realize that others, to some degree, always see you through their own needs. What they cannot accept in others is often what they cannot accept in themselves.

I felt rejected by my parents' behavior. They seemed to withhold the love and approval I desired. I responded with projections of bitterness, belligerent behavior, manipulations, justifiable revenge, and a general sense of guilt brought about by self-hatred. I was blameless. Or was I? I now believe that they understood the need for love but they lacked the power to give the intellectual and emotional intimacy I sought.

These projections, this self-deception, prevented me from looking within and taking responsibility for my own actions, and I projected this learned behavior onto others. There is no end to man's self-deception, because whatever he is going to do he can always rationalize.

> One day a man boasted in the bar that he was a man of iron will and now he would show it by not touching alcohol again in his life. But not even a day could pass. In the evening he came to the bar and said loudly for all to hear. "I am stronger than my willpower! I fought the whole day and finally conquered my damn willpower! A double Scotch please!"

Man is strange, very strange, because he begins by trying to deceive others and ends up by deceiving himself.

> The wise are caught in their own craftiness and their words are but in vain.

I now perceive my anger was a hidden desire for unselfish love and understanding from my parents. They rarely gave this love unless I forced the issue and at times behaved as a child.

These unfulfilled desires are contaminations and addictions of the past, and I am desperately trying to change them to preferences and not feel victimized if I feel my needs have not been met.

What I perceived as a normal condition in the past was nothing but a sickness. My eventual freedom from the past will be achieved through total Self-awareness and Self-acceptance.

> ...and you shall know the truth and the
> truth shall set you free.
>
> John 8:32

Only as man surrenders himself to divine love will he find truth and become free.

> He who humbles himself shall be saved.
> He who bends shall be made straight.
> He who empties himself shall be filled.

One is not to make the self free; on the contrary, one has to be free from the self (ego). Everyone has to find the Truth for himself. The Truth is not mind! The Truth is not action! The Truth is of "Being." It is not a question of doing. It is simply a question of "Being."

My family, of an authoritarian and fiercely competitive nature, took advantage of my disposition. My repressed anger affected me to the point of depression.

I reluctantly went to a psychiatrist and was told that my depression was caused by a chemical imbalance, and that I would need antidepressant medication for the rest of my life. He also made me aware of the cause of my actions and the reality of my family situation.

My parents were unaware of the effects that their actions were having upon my feelings and general welfare. My brothers were also unaware or possibly unconcerned about how their actions were affecting our relationship, one that I was desperately trying to maintain. My efforts to make them aware of their lack of concern towards respecting my integrity and our parents' wishes, feelings, and general welfare over the years proved fruitless.

He that troubleth his own house shall inherit the wind.

Proverbs 11:29

A good name is to be more desired than great riches.

Proverbs 22:1

I was told that I must understand the cause and the effects that their actions had upon my emotional well-being and take responsibility only for my own actions and cope with them the best I could. It was at that time I wrote my first poem, "A Paradox."

A PARADOX
For Those Who See

Games are played and games are fought,
Depending on the prize that's sought.
Played by rules from different books,
Some played by fools who do not look.

Ethics and morals are for ones such as we,
Winning without them would not give us glee.
The loss of respect for those so dear,
Will they lose our love, is what I fear.

An unfair advantage is taken by those,
Who grew up and confided in all our woes.
Reckless and ruthless wherever they go,
Knowing our weaknesses, they strike a hard blow.

The absence of God is all their reward,
For those who live and die by the sword.
In business or pleasure their goals should be,
Winning with love and respect for Thee.

It is difficult to accept and hard to understand,
To see it inflicted upon one's fellow man.
Is winning really winning from ones such as we?
An interesting paradox for those who see.

The essence of man's being is eternal truth and perfect love that transcend the paradoxes of life.

The way of paradoxes is the way of Truth.

What was driving me? Nothing seemed to satisfy me anymore. Like everyone else, I wanted to succeed. I had built many structures that were the envy of the community; and, as time passed, I continued to seek money, power, prestige, and whatever favorite phantoms I desired at the time. Such activities were only veils against despair.

Why do you look without for that which is within you?

Meister Eckhart

I made new friends and began to miss the old ones that had died. They were all very dear to me.

Around the corner I have a friend,
In this great city that has no end.
Yet days go by and weeks rush on,
And before I know it a year is gone.
And I never see my old friend's face,
For life is a swift and terrible race.
He knows I like him just as well
As in the days when I rang his bell
An he rang mine. We were younger then,
And now we are busy, tired men—
Tired with playing a foolish game,
Tired with trying to make a name.
"Tomorrow," I say, "I will call on Jim,
Just to show that I'm thinking of him."

But tomorrow comes and tomorrow goes,
And the distance between us grows and grows,
Around the corner—yet miles away—
"Here's a telegram, sir,"—"Jim died today."
And that's what we get, and deserve in the end—
Around the corner, a vanishing friend.[13]

After they had passed away I realized that they were more precious than gold and that I had taken them all for granted. I also became aware that I would never see them again or be able to show them any love and appreciation for all that they had done and meant to me. I have now come to the realization that because of their kindness and generosity, I have an obligation to repay this debt in kind.

Make new friends, but keep the old;
These are silver, those are gold.
New-made friendships, like new wine
Age will mellow and refine.

Friendships that have stood the test—
Time and change—are surely best;
Brow may wrinkle, hair grow gray,
Friendship never knows decay.

For 'mid old friends, tried and true,
Once more we our youth renew.
But old friends, also, may die;
New friends must their place supply.

Cherish friendship in your breast—
New is good, but old is best.
Make new friends, but keep the old;
These are silver, those are gold.[10]

I was left with an empty feeling that forced me to begin my quest for something greater than that which I had been seeking, something that I was not able to put into words. Through sheer weariness with trying to satisfy my insatiable desire I began to look elsewhere for fulfillment. Only when I was absolutely convinced that living in the ordinary sense does not bring true happiness, security, or peace did it occur to me that I had been searching for fulfillment in the wrong places.

The material world would make one comfortable, but it would not bring love, peace, and true happiness. I now wanted desperately to learn and to succeed; not necessarily in the terms of what the world called success, because somehow I had lost confidence in the accepted values of society. I knew if I did find what I was looking for, it would come from within and it would be something that I would share with others. But how was I to find it, and where?

> Ask, and it will be given you;
> Seek, and you will find;
> Knock, and it will be opened to you.
>
> For every one who asks receives,
> And he who seeks finds,
> And to him who knocks it will be opened.
>
> Matthew 7:7-8
>
> Behold I stand at the door and knock. He who hears My voice and opens the door, I will come in to Him......
>
> Revelation 3:20

One night I had a dream that gave me infinite peace, tranquility, and happiness. In the dream I saw my Uncle Bill. He was a passenger in a red convertible driving down the street. All I could see of the driver was that he had a halo over his head.

I quickly rushed out the door and chased after my uncle. He left the car and went into his house. I knocked on the door and, when my aunt answered, I said, "Where is Uncle Bill?" She replied, "You know that your Uncle Bill has been dead for years." I then woke up and when I realized that this peace and love that I was experiencing was only a dream, I cried.

I quickly picked up a pencil and the most convenient piece of paper to write on, and proceeded to write this poem:

The Angel and the Peacock

There came to me in a dream so rare
A vision of love for an angel fair;
The glory of a peacock in days gone by,
So sad to see that time must fly.

Love's precious moments in the space of time
Must be appreciated like a glass of wine;
Enjoy your days with joy and bliss,
It may again be a time as this.

After I finished, I discovered that I had written it on the back of a Christmas card that had a picture of Joseph leading a donkey with Mary on it and baby Jesus cradled in her arms.

Years passed and a friend died. When I broke the unfortunate news to one of our friends, he took it hard. I told him that our deceased friend was far better off now than before, because of his suffering and all the serious problems he had had during his lifetime. I was told that my philosophy was "absurd, that when you are dead you are dead, and that is all there is to it!"

I told this friend of mine that if I believed as he did I would wish our friend back with all his pain and suffering. Another friend of mine at that time heard me make this statement and asked me to write a poem that would adequately express my feelings. This is the poem I wrote at that time:

IMMORTALITY
"Eternal Love"

We search when young, we search when old,
All search to find an intangible goal.
Thoughts of love and spirits bright
Bring joys and beauties of heaven in sight.

Feasts of silver and feasts of Gold,
Greed and envy hide the soul.
Toil and sweat, grief and pain,
Misery and hunger will not remain.

Time will come when all must die,
And find their soul at evening's tide.
With this spirit, the search will cease,
For this love is God, eternal peace.

Many more years passed and a voice within me said, "Is this all there is?" I traveled until I realized that this was not the answer I was looking for, so I settled down in luxury and leisure. It must have been about this time in my life when this voice within me said, "There must be more," so I made up my mind to devote as much time and effort to finding the reason and purpose of life as I had done in creating a successful business. My desire for information now was eager and the search for Truth honest, sincere, and persistent.

According to the strength of your inquiring
spirit will be the depth of your enlightenment.

In my newly found freedom of luxury and leisure, I had many friends who gave as well as suggested many enlightening books that I should read. I had a lot of free time for studies, so I read most of the day and often into the night as well. They also suggested various classes that they thought I would like to attend and places to go that would expand and broaden my spiritual Self-awareness. At first I was reluctant but I began with a few consciousness-awareness courses.

The Experience of Meditation

At one of these classes I was told by the instructor, a retired Jewish surgeon who had survived the holocaust, that if we could get about twelve people together, he would guide us through a unique course in music meditation. He said that we would experience through this meditation the inner dimension of our soul and assured us that this meditation experience would surpass all understanding.

We formed this group and I went to the first meeting with a friend and his wife, who had encouraged me in pursuing a better understanding of myself.

The instructor told us to lie on the floor and relax. He turned off the light and turned on some meditation music and proceeded to guide us through mental visualizations that would bring us to a state of peaceful inner realization. The music stopped, the lights were turned on, and we sat up. The instructor asked if any one had had an inner experience. One individual stated that he was drawn up into the universe and saw an array of colors and beauty. Another person said that he was in a desert and was absorbed in its beauty.

I looked at my friends in bewilderment and, as we were driving home, they asked me what I thought. I said I thought they were crazy! I asked my friend and his wife what they thought and they said that they agreed and wanted to know whether I was going again the following week. I replied that I was and they asked me why. I told them that I was willing to go again, because it was relaxing and I had nothing better to do. We all continued going for awhile. After a few weeks my friend and his wife dropped out, and I kept going by myself.

As time passed I also began to meditate at home; and one night, while in bed, I began to meditate with sounds of music that reflected every day happenings that we seem to ignore while we are busy chasing shadows and our favorite phantoms. The sounds were of music, rain, wind, heartbeats, thunder, and other such vibrations.

All of a sudden, I became aware of my inner existence and a peace came over me as I gazed at an inner galaxy of stars and colors. The peace that came over me was the peace that I experienced in the dream that had inspired me to write the poem, "The Angel and the Peacock." My wife was lying next to me at the time, and I said to her, "You will not believe it! It is beautiful!" When I said that, it all began to fade away and disappear. No matter how hard I tried that night, I could not bring that inner vision back.

Faith Healing

Another time a friend of mine asked if I wished to go with her to a faith healer. I was reluctant and very suspicious, but again, since I had nothing better to do, I went. When we arrived, there was a lady stretched out on a table. She claimed that she was in pain. A group of people gathered around her and began laying their hands on her body in order to channel their energies to heal the pain. Again I thought these people were crazy. I sat down, hoping that the session would end so I could leave.

One of the instructors, sensing my embarrassment, came up to me and asked if I would like to work with her on a one-to-one basis. Reluctantly I agreed. She told me that she was suffering an ailment, and if I took my hands and moved them slightly above her body I would be able to feel the heat that was caused by her pain.

I followed her instruction with no effect. She sensed that I felt stupid, said that I should not be embarrassed, and asked me to try again. I experienced the same result. She mentioned to me that, as I was moving my hand slightly above her body I should change my consciousness.

This struck a responsive cord, because when I meditate I do change my consciousness. Not a consciousness that directs its attention to each individual thing, but rather a consciousness that goes beyond heaven and earth, beyond the substance of the world and the weight of mortality.

When ordinary consciousness is transcended, we enter the sanctuary where God and the soul touch: the very core of the Self, where the perceptions of the world and its multiplicity totally vanish, and only the divine union between the soul and God exists.

So I decided to try again, and this time I felt substantial heat coming from her shoulder. I moved my hands away from this area to other parts of her body. She asked if I had felt anything. I told her that I had not. I do not know why I said that, because it was not true. It may have been because I did not want to believe that I was also one of those "misguided" people that I had condemned so severely.

I asked if I could try again and proceeded to do so. Again, I felt the heat emanating from the same area. She asked me if I had felt anything. This time I said, "Yes," because I was sure of what I had experienced. She asked me to tell her where the pain was coming from. Being of a suspicious nature, I asked her to tell me first. She said it was in her right shoulder, in the exact place where I had felt an above-normal amount of body heat present. I did not know what to think. Was I also losing my sense of reality? As I was leaving, the lady on the table claimed that her pain was gone. She was thankful to all those who had channelled their energies into curing her ailment. What was I to think?

Visualizing an Aura

Another time I was with a group of people, when one of them asked if anyone had ever seen an aura. We all said we had not, and asked if she had. She said that she had and proceeded to instruct us so we also could see one. I was again very suspicious.

She stood against a clear wall and asked us to stare at her. No one saw an aura. She asked us to stare past her. We again saw nothing until she said that we should change our consciousness. This time I stared past and beyond her—a consciousness not of heaven and earth, but one of going beyond the mind to a complete annihilation of the world and its sense of multiplicity.

At that moment an aura formed around her; and, to my surprise, I saw a radiance of light coming from her head. Only one other person had a similar experience at that time. I could not wait to tell my wife; but, when I arrived home and described what had happened, she laughed. I was unmoved by her disbelief. I asked her to stand against the wall so I could look for her aura. Not only did I see the aura around her head, but the aura radiated from her head like icicles, similar to those I have seen in many pictures of saints. This observation made me realize that these artists may not have been drawing the auras in their pictures from their imagination, but from what they had really seen.

Illusion

Another time when I was meditating, I stared at a flower and realized what some artists see in their perception of form and color. While in a deep meditative state of contemplation I could see the beauty of the flower and the brilliance of its colors in an exaggerated and distorted form, much like Paul Gauguin's paintings and Vincent Van Gogh's "Sunflower." The flower was radiantly beautiful and I came to realize that beauty is a reflection in the eyes of the beholder, and that what seemed to be real, may be a configuration of our imagination, an illusion, or aspects of a heavenly body, all a matter of our perception.

Annihilation

I remember being present at a particular house party which was attended by many guests. While moving around and listening to them I realized that their conversations were senseless and useless. Their egos were in bloom, for all they talked about was golf, tennis, money, power, sex, and so forth. This in itself is not bad, but when it consumes and dominates one's life to the point that one plays golf or tennis three times a day every day, in my opinion, is a sickness. I realized that this was not the answer I was looking for. No one cared or talked about anything but himself.

When I was leaving I saw a beautiful flower by the walkway and stared at it. Then to my surprise, I lost all sense of reality and my consciousness became that flower. I would not tell this to anyone for fear I would surely be thought crazy.

This experience made more sense to me when I enrolled at N.Y.U. and read the book, *"The Variety of Religious Experiences"* by William James. He documented cases of others who had had similar experiences. My experiences were validated by those who came before me. I knew now that I was not crazy. One could not be crazy and have had such a fulfilling experience.

Various Forms of God-Consciousness

In one of the books I read, there was a man in prison that made friends with a rat as well as a fly. It was difficult for me to believe that a fly had a consciousness that would be able to communicate with a man.

He told about how a fly landed on his knee and how he made friends with it. The fly moved its head and the man moved his to conform with that of the fly. The fly then moved its head the other way. The man did the same. This went on for awhile. The man then placed his finger on his thigh, moving it back and forth with the movements of the fly. Then gradually he moved his finger closer and closer to the fly.

At times the fly would fly away but it would always return. He would repeat the procedure until his finger came close to the fly. He then would leave his finger near the fly and wait. After awhile the fly climbed onto the man's finger. The fly felt confident enough to walk around without any fear.

Just as I had finished this book, a fly landed on my knee. I thought a bit and felt I would try to duplicate his experience. I had heard of how animals felt safe with Saint Francis of Assisi and wondered if it could be done with a fly as I had read in this book. I followed the same procedure. The fly moved its head; I moved mine. This went on for awhile. I placed my finger on my thigh and gradually moved it towards the fly. The fly flew away.

I waited and wondered if it would come back. It did and I moved my finger closer. The fly flew away again. This went on for quite some time until I placed my finger near the fly and waited. It did not move, and neither did I. After a period of time it started to walk around and then climbed on my finger. I lifted my hand and looked it directly in the eye, and it did not move. I watched in amazement as it started to walk around on my finger. The fly then flew away.

Later my wife came in and started chasing something around the room with a magazine in her hand. I asked her what she was doing, and she said that she was trying to kill a fly. She said that a fly had landed on the lamp shade next to me, and that I should kill it. When I turned and looked at it, to my surprise, it was the same fly that I had made friends with.

Jokingly I told my wife that I could not kill it, because this particular fly was a friend of mine. She laughed and then I proceeded to tell her what I had read in the book about the man who had made friends with a fly, and how I followed the same procedure and experienced the same results. She laughed even louder and said, "Let me see you do it now." I really doubted that I could do it again, but I reached up and placed my finger next to the fly and to my and my wife's amazement the fly climbed onto my finger.

A few days later my daughter walked into the room and I related this story to her. Both she and my wife laughed and thought it was just a coincidence. At that moment a fly landed on the bed. Both my daughter and my wife wanted to see me do it again. I looked at the fly and found it was the same fly. I placed my finger near it and it quickly climbed on my finger, to our mutual amazement. Then we were all caught up in laughter.

As you can see, my doubting in the past that proved ungrounded changed my way of thinking and perceiving things. Now if someone said that he could walk on water, I would not be too quick to doubt that it could be done, although I must admit I would have to see it or experience it for myself before I truly believed it. But I surely would not discount the fact that it could be possible.

A Cosmic Vision or an Out-of-body Experience?

When I was a young boy I had an unusual experience. I was lying in bed and I sat up and turned around and noticed that my body was still lying in bed asleep. This frightened me, so I quickly laid back down into my body, then sat up again. Wide-awake, I looked around and noticed that I was not lying in bed, but sitting up thinking that what I had experienced must have been a dream.

Later in my life this happened to me again; I was sitting in the corner of my cocktail lounge after a long and tedious day's work. The cocktail lounge was very busy. Everyone was singing and having a good time. I was contemplating what had transpired that day and observing the joy and laughter that permeated the room.

All of a sudden I realized that I was seeing everything that was going on in the room including myself sitting in the corner, from a vantage point far above the room. This was a peaceful feeling and when I was nudged by one of my employees, I realized that this perception was not real and that I must have dozed off. What I had experienced must have been a dream.

Now that I have lived and experienced many unusual events that gave me reason to pause, I question whether they were dreams or a change of consciousness that enabled me in a contemplative moment to perceive what was happening from another state of consciousness.

In retrospect, I feel that these two experiences were not dreams. They puzzle the mind but not the heart. Man lives in two realities and must recognize the duality of his nature. Beyond duality is a center of consciousness, and in that consciousness the source of all forces of existence is reached.

I experienced something as being different from myself when I saw myself apart from the person I was looking at. If you stand apart from yourself—that is, from the body-mind complex—you see that you are not that body. You are consciousness alone, and in you the whole creation exists. What I thought was an out-of-body experience must have been a cosmic vision seen through the consciousness of God.

Love Your Enemies

It was said, in the first consciousness-awareness class that I attended, that one should love his enemy. This was difficult for me to comprehend. How can one love his enemy? I was told that if I did not love my enemy, it would be I who would suffer. I sat back and thought this remark was absurd. I spoke up again and wanted to know, if someone killed someone dear to me, how could I not hate him? I was told that hating anyone is like burning down your own house to git rid of a rat. It would drastically affect the quality of my life. I was also told that Jesus said, "Love your Enemies." At that time this statement seemed to me to be irresponsible.

> But I say unto you, Love your enemies, bless
> them that curse you, do good to them that
> hate you, and persecute you;
>
> Matthew 5:44

While I was talking to a friend of mine, whose son had died at the age of twelve, I told her about the classes I had attended that professed that you should love your enemy. We discussed it, then our conversation led to the subject of love. She said that after her son had died she suffered for years, until she came to the realization that she had his love and sweet companionship here on earth for twelve years, and that this love transcended the suffering and gave her peace.

Her suffering must have ceased when she accepted that which only God alone can see and is unrevealed until its season. She realized that she now has his (His) love within her heart to this day, a love that one can never forget.

When I gave this some thought I said, "You know, we are our own worst enemies and we create our own suffering by the way we perceive things." She then pointed her finger at me and said, "There, love yourself!" Now loving myself made more sense then loving my enemy.

Love thy neighbor as thyself.

Leviticus19:18

Love your neighbor for he is yourself.

Buddha

I had another friend who had a similar experience. She told me when her daughter died as a child, she had blamed God for taking her. My friend had suffered for years and was tormented by a recurring dream.

She dreamed that her daughter was buried on top of a steep hill with a cross over her grave. It was raining and everything was as black as ink. She tried to climb the hill to be with her daughter, but for some reason she was unable to move. She was struck by lightning and was sure she was going to die. She pleaded and prayed, "God, please help me!" At that moment she saw a rainbow over the cross and under the rainbow was written, "In God we Trust." That night she experienced a love within her heart that transcended the suffering and gave her peace.

I came to the realization that one must love in an inner sense. "I love that person out of the overflowing love within myself." God's love is poured out with such extravagant generosity that whoever fails to respond to it is simply self-condemned.

We meet the enemy and we are them.

Transcendence of Good and Evil

I had an occasion to tell a friend of mine what I considered to be a truth. There is no right or wrong, good or evil, but only the experience and the way that experience is perceived.

He became upset with that statement and told me that it was not so. He was of Jewish ancestry and proceeded to explain to me the evils of the holocaust, where six million innocent people were put to death. "Now that is evil!" he replied. "How can it be perceived any other way?"

I was taken back by his agitation and defense of what he considered an irresponsible statement coming from me. I gave it some thought and, after further consideration, told him that he had a valid point. I would have to give it more thought before I could come up with an adequate and intelligent response to my statement, or concede that my initial remark was false.

I went home and read whatever I could find on the subject and concluded that life is a paradox. Love and Hate. Good and Evil. Right and Wrong. Fall and Redemption. Sin and Forgiveness. Death and Renewal. A world of opposites with boundaries.

The mind creates these boundaries, depending on our perception, and is seen by the enlightened mind as dual aspects of the Truth that lies beyond the Paradox.

> The truest sayings are paradoxical.   Taoism

If one suffers and is not transformed by his suffering, then the evil will be perceived as evil. If one suffers and is transformed, then this evil, this suffering, will be perceived as good—a means to a glorious end.

The statement that I made to my friend, that there is no right or wrong, good or evil, but only the experience, and the way that experience is perceived, would be confusing to most people unless their life's suffering fostered the awareness that brought about their redemption. A transformation that changes the heart and gives it new birth.

> I live with evil while my self is here;
> With God both self and evil disappear.[1]

The Grace of God

I once asked my mother if she loved my father, and she said that she did. I asked her if she loved God, and she said that she did. Then I asked her whom she loved more and she replied, "I love God more, because if I did not love God, how could I love your father?"

> He who loves father or mother more than me is not worthy of me;
> And he who loves son or daughter more than me is not worthy of me;
> And he who does not take his cross and follow after me is not worthy of me.
> He who has found his life shall lose it, and he who has lost his life for my sake shall find it.
>
> Matthew 10:37-39

The personal love for Caesar, mother, father, husband, wife, son, or daughter is just symbolic of the concentrated state of devotion to God. A man can live without Caesar, mother, father, husband, wife, son, or daughter, but he cannot live without God, apart and estranged from his true nature. How could one love anything if one did not love God first?

> And thou shalt love the Lord thy God with all thine heart, and with all thy soul, and with all thy might.
>
> Deuteronomy 6:5

I asked my mother how she felt about my father, who doubted the existence of God, and she said that it was his concern. One must find God for himself.

> This day before dawn I ascended a hill and look'd at the crowded heaven.
> And I said to my spirit, "When we become the enfolders of those orbs and the pleasure and knowledge of everything in them shall we be fill'd and satisfied then?"
> And my spirit said, "No, we but level that lift to pass and continue beyond."
> You are also asking me questions and I hear you, I answer that I can not answer, you must find out yourself.
>
> "Song of Myself"
> Walt Whitman

Pass me not, O gentle Savior, Hear my humble cry;
While on others Thou art calling, Do not pass me by.
Let me at a throne of mercy, Find a sweet relief;
Kneeling there in deep contrition, Help my unbelief.

Trusting only in Thy merit, Would I seek Thy face;
Heal my wounded broken spirit, Save me by Thy grace.
Thou the Spring of all my comfort, More than life to me,
Whom have I on earth beside Thee? Whom in Heav'n but Thee?

> Savior, Savior, Hear my humble cry;
> While on others Thou art calling,
> Do not pass me by.[11]

When my family and I were vacationing at the ocean, I felt that I had failed to find the meaning and purpose of life. I told that to my wife and said that I felt life was senseless and useless—a temporal sense of futility, one of chasing our favorite phantoms and slaying the mind's illusionary dragons.

> Alone, alone, all, all alone,
> Alone on a wide wide sea!
> And never a saint took pity on
> My soul in agony.[2]

All life had to offer was an endless array of pain and suffering within the delusions of man's folly.

> A thousand screams the heavens smote;
> And every scream tore through my throat.
> No hurt I did not feel, no death
> That was not mine; mine each last breath
> That, crying, met an answering cry
> From the compassion that was I.
> All suffering mine, and mine its rod;
> Mine, pity like the pity of God.
> Ah, awful weight! Infinity.
>
> For my omniscience I paid toll
> In infinite remorse of soul.
> All sin was of my sinning, all
> Atoning mine, and mine the gall

Of all regret. Mine was the weight
Of every brooded wrong, the hate
That stood behind each envious thrust,
Mine every greed, mine every lust.
And all the while for every grief,
Each suffering, I craved relief
With individual desire,___ [3]

A curse, an agony for all mankind, and nothing seemed to give me true satisfaction.

The many men, so beautiful!
And they all dead did lie:
And a thousand thousand things
Lived on; and so did I. [2]

That evening when I was at our cottage looking at the beautiful full moon over the ocean and observing the sea oats in the sand dunes, I spoke to a God whom I never believed in and said, "I have done all that I can! If you do exist, please help me! There is no more that I can do. The rest is up to You."

For whosoever shall call upon the name of
the Lord shall be saved."

Romans 10:13

Suddenly at that moment a universal tide of love flowed in upon me in waves of joy and gladness. Every longing of the heart was satisfied. I learned at that moment a grand lesson: that suffering is the price which must be paid for all that is worth having.

The hardships and tragedies which befall man from time to time are all for the purpose of teaching him lessons which he has refused to learn in any other way.

I shall lead my beloved into the desert and I
shall speak into her heart.

I shall lead the noble soul into solitude and
their I shall speak to her heart.[4]

My soul dissolved and melted away
when my beloved spoke.

But as many as have received Him, to them
He gave the right to become children of God.

John 1:12

I had a personal revelation that day which brought
about a total conversion—a revelation that fostered
within me love and compassion. I saw a radiant light
and experienced a love that will guide me for the rest of
my life. When the experience had passed, it was the
basis for my faith. To believe in it, to hold on to it, to be
comforted by it, and to trust it.

Amazing Grace, how sweet the sound,
That saved a soul like me.
I once was lost but now am found;
Was blind but now I see.

'Twas Grace that taught my heart to fear,
And Grace my fears relieved;
How precious did that Grace appear.
The hour I first believed.[12]

At that very moment I experienced an inner peace
that cannot adequately be expressed in words. I had
never before experienced anything like it. My heart was
empty and at the same time full of bliss of eternal
solitude.

O happy living things! no tongue
Their beauty might declare:
A spring of love gush'd from my heart,
And I blessed them unaware:
Sure my kind saint took pity on me,
And I blessed them unaware.

> The self-same moment I could pray;
> And from my neck so free
> The Albatross fell off, and sank
> Like lead into the sea.[2]

I thought that I had been released from my body, that I was suspended in mid-air. All the things that had been confused before suddenly became very clear to me. I had a sense of knowledge more than human. I felt that I had broken away and was free, and felt that if it lasted another minute, I would die. And yet I was willing to die if I could hold onto it, because for that one moment I had the feeling that God and I were One.

> But soon there breathed a wind on me,
> Nor sound nor motion made:
> Its path was not upon the sea,
> In ripple or in shade.

> It raised my hair, it fanned my cheek
> Like a meadow-gale of spring—
> It mingled strangely with my fears,
> Yet it felt like a welcoming.[2]

Worldly ambitions and cares died in the light of that glorious truth. One long song of love and peace.

> A spring of love gushed from my heart
> And I blessed them unaware:
> Sure my kind saint took pity on me.
> And I blessed them unaware.[2]

It was a love that transcended time and space. There was no subject or object. I ceased to exist.

> In merging of itself in God the spirit passes
> away.

I did not exist. Or did I? I quickly picked up a pencil and a piece of paper and in that transcendental state of consciousness I wrote this poem:

REBIRTH
Enlightenment
An Elevated State of Consciousness

A Full—majestic moon
   Radiates a beauty,
Over the vast turbulent sea.
   A veil is lifted!—A soul is free!—
To walk the beach in radiant light.
   A spirit that blows across the water,
Stirring up the waves as—
   A heart is stirred by the thoughts of love,
Moving the ocean—to the shore—
   With waves that pulsate a desire to be—
Sea oats—in the sand dunes of time.
   Swaying—Reaching—
For the warmth of the Sun,
   A longing to procreate,
A reunion with——————GOD—

I had a glimpse of eternity. The inner certainty of eternal bliss. For one brief moment the veil was lifted and the struggle had ceased. I did not know how empty my soul was until it was filled.

I truly feel that I did not write this poem. The heavenly powers brought this poem down to earth. I was merely the agent of its birth. This poem was one of free verse and I never cared for poetry that was written in free verse. All my other poetry rhymed. Most of my poems took me days to write and I knew that this poem came from beyond and existed before time. I was a bamboo and God made a golden flute of me.

   And now 'twas like all instruments,
   Now like a lonely flute,
   And now it is an angel's song,
   That makes the Heavens be mute.[2]

After a few months passed, I realized that I had not taken any antidepressant medication for quite some time. I then realized that I had stopped taking the medication on that night I experienced complete fulfillment. I was absorbed in a love beyond description.

> He went like one that hath been stunned,
> And is of sense forlorn:
> A sadder and wiser man,
> He rose the morrow morn.[2]

What joy, what pain and sorrow that was the cause and occasion of so great a redemption lifts one to accept the pain and suffering of the human condition.

> I know not how such things can be;
> I only know there came to me
> A fragrance such as never clings
> To aught save happy living things;
> A sound as of some joyous elf
> Singing sweet songs to please himself,
> And through and over everything,
> A sense of glad awakening.
>
> And as I looked a quickening gust
> Of wind blew up to me and thrust
> Into my face a miracle
> Of orchard breath, and with the smell,—
> I know how such things can be!—
> I breathed my soul back into me.
> Ah! Up then from the ground sprang I
> And hailed the earth with such a cry
> As is not heard save from a man
> Who has been dead, and lives again.[3]

It was at this point in my soul's evolution that the sleeping wisdom within me stirred and experienced an awakening. The enlightenment was the result of the ultimate expansion of my consciousness. I had grasped the infinite wisdom of the universal mind.

> O God, I cried, no dark disguise
> Can e'er hereafter hide from me
> Thy radiant identity![3]

When our ordinary mind, our usual consciousness, is expanded or elevated to a higher state, it leads to an increased perception and awareness, resulting in the realization that man is Spirit and not just passions of the mind.

I was very fortunate, because by the grace of God the infinite beauty of the world was revealed to me. I had a glimpse of heaven, one of divine bliss.

Now I believe I understand what these following sayings mean, "Before I became enlightened, mountains were mountains and rivers were rivers. During enlightenment, mountains are not mountains, rivers are not rivers. And after enlightenment, mountains again become mountains and rivers become rivers."

My comprehension of this statement is that before enlightenment I saw the world as it was, as many objects—the mountains were only mountains and the rivers were only rivers. During enlightenment there is no subject or object. The mountains and rivers do not exist. Only God exists. When God rules supreme, the laws of nature are suspended altogether. After enlightenment you again see the world as it is, but now you see beyond the objects of perception in a non-conceptual state of existence. The mountains are more than mountains and the rivers are more than rivers, because now you see them through the eyes of God.

Once you experience God, you are forever changed. Had anyone told me that this would happen to me, I would not have believed him. I saw more than I can tell, and I understood more than I saw. No concepts can reach it; no understanding can grasp it. How can one describe a thing that has not entered through the senses?

> To him who has had the experience no explanation is necessary; to him who has not, none is possible.

The memory and experience of that moment (that sense of Joy, that vision of His divine beauty) now gives me true faith and the experience will remain with me fresh and vivid until the day I die.

> Blessed assurance, Jesus is mine!
> O what a foretaste of glory divine!
> Heir of salvation, purchase of God,
> Born of His Spirit, Washed in His blood.
>
> Perfect submission, perfect delight,
> Visions of rapture now burst on my sight,
> Angels descending, bring from above,
> Echoes of mercy, whispers of love.
>
> Perfect submission, all is at rest,
> I in my Saviour am happy and blessed,
> Watching and waiting, looking above,
> Filled with His goodness, lost in his love.

Love of Self

This love consumed me. When I came to my senses I finally realized how one could truly love his enemy. I misunderstood the phrase, "Love your enemy." One must be loving to his enemy. It is a state of being. It is your birthright. It is like a flower that gives off its fragrance to the just and the unjust. It brought to mind, Ralph Waldo Emerson's poem:

The Rhodora

On Being Asked, Whence Is the Flower

Rhodora! if the sages ask thee why
This charm is wasted on the earth and sky,
Tell them, dear, that if eyes were made for seeing
Then Beauty is its own excuse for being.

Beauty needs no explanation. It has a divine right to sovereignty. Love is always there. Love is inexhaustible. It is the universal kiss. If you make yourself available, God will kiss you.

Every flower in the garden praises God. Every leaf and petal radiates the wisdom of God. If man will only look behind all created beauty, he will see and witness the source of eternal beauty.

You must be centered in love. To withhold love, regardless of the reason, is to withhold the mental power by which you can be healthy, happy, and successful.

The internal core of truth is the expression of love. It is an attitude in you. You love your enemy with the overflowing love within yourself. You must love in an inner sense. Do not turn off that flow of love. Be centered in love.

As the lily will grow upon a heap of rubbish, one should shine forth by His wisdom among the people that walk in darkness.

Love and compassion are like flowers in the desert. No one knows that they have flowered and are giving off perfume. It is just being given. The flower has bloomed, so the fragrance is there. When one has freedom, he also has love. This love is compassion. He is completely open and giving every moment. If someone passes and becomes aware of its presence, he may receive it. When love and compassion are there, it is up to you whether you are able to receive them or not.

One can give love or withhold it from you only if the relationship is of the mind and not of the heart. Love is a divine reality when there is no separation, no love-hate relationship. True love and compassion do not exist if one is able to withhold them. True love and compassion are centered in the heart, and love is forever expressing itself.

Projection. The Enemy Within

I now wanted to know more. I wanted to know what had happened to me. My nature had changed. From that time on I gained humility. I had become conscious of my own shortcomings and, because of that awareness, I had love and compassion for the suffering of others. I saw their weaknesses for the first time as projections of the faults that I possessed.

> I have seen my own behavior in you and I cannot bear the sight.

What you think of others is basically what you think of yourself. A thief thinks everyone is a thief. Whatever you think I am or want me to be, that is what I am to you. We cannot stand other people having the same faults as ourselves.

> Axiom.......that one hates in others those things and only those things that one hates in oneself.

We must make a serious effort to become aware of our own faults and transgressions. We must look within ourselves, take responsibility for our own actions, and stop trying to correct the faults of others. We must stop trying to convince ourselves that it is only they who are wrong.

A Drunkard Accuses a Drunkard

A sot became extremely drunk—his legs
And head sank listless, weighed by wine's thick dregs.
A sober neighbour put him in a sack
And took him homewards hoisted on his back.
Another drunk went stumbling by the first,
Who woke and stuck his head outside and cursed.
"Hey, you, you lousy dipsomaniac,"
He yelled as he was borne off in the sack,
"If you'd had fewer drinks, just two or three,
You would be walking now as well as me."
He saw the other's state but not his own,
And in this blindness he is not alone;
You cannot love, and this is why you seek
To find men vicious, or depraved, or weak—
If you could search for love and persevere
The sins of other men would disappear.[1]

Man's hatred is often projected upon the person who makes him conscious of his own bad qualities. One sees the speck in one's eye as a log in the eye of one's brother.

> And why do you look at the speck that is in your brother's eye, but do not notice the log that is in your own eye?
> Or how can you say to your brother, "Let me take the speck out of your eye," and behold, the log is in your own eye?
> You hypocrite, first take the log out of your own eye, and then you will see clearly to take the speck out of your brother's eye.

> Luke 6:41-42

Claim your God, "Being," your divine center. It is your birthright. It is the magnificent splendor within you. Live in excellence, so that others seeing this

52

excellence may rise to a higher level of God-consciousness. Be the man through whom you wish to influence others. Your brother, seeing this transformation of light, will cast the speck out of his own eye and be a light unto himself. You must be centered in a higher state of God-consciousness in order to be able to soar into the heavens.

If one is to gradually transform the world and effectively make changes in it, he must transcend and liberate himself in his own way from the involvements of this world. He must first find his true Self, his (His) true nature, and with this spirit set an example that is worthy to be followed.

> Our Father which art in heaven, Hallowed be thy name. Thy kingdom come. Thy will be done on earth, as it is in heaven. Give us this day our daily bread. And forgive us our debts, as we forgive our debtors. And lead us not into temptation, but deliver us from evil: For thine is the kingdom, and the power, and the glory, for ever.
>
> Matthew 6:9-13

The images we project in our minds over the years are the blueprints by which we mold our own destinies. The destinies of men are subject to unchangeable laws that must fulfill themselves. Man has it in his power to shape his own destiny, according to the behavior he shows towards the influences of these benevolent and destructive forces.

> It was the face of my own evil shadow that I saw and found in others because I did not wish to face it within myself.

I realized that humility made me conscious of my faults, and that everything that existed was of a finite nature in time and space. This awareness fostered understanding, love, and compassion for others. I became aware of my sins and weaknesses. Without such knowledge one cannot have a change of heart and truly be humbled and forgiving of the faults and transgressions of others, and, indeed, find peace within himself. For if you forgive men their trespasses, your heavenly Father also will forgive you.

> As man thinketh in his heart so is he, and
> Where a man's heart is, there will his treasure be.

We know in all humility our transgressions. We become aware of the pomp and vanity of this pretentious world in its empty affections and pernicious pride. This awareness fosters humility, compassion, and love from the ground of our being for all nature's kind. We realize what we are by nature and by grace. Only through grace is man made like unto God and shares in His divinity.

We know that we are one and co-creators with God. Humility is a work of the indwelling Spirit's mercy and grace. We need the light of Grace to know our sins and weaknesses, and to experience His presence.

I experienced a Presence guiding me and discovered that when I went against this Presence I created suffering for myself. I then came to the realization that it was God who was guiding me, and it was my ego that was causing my suffering and separating me from His love, Presence, and guidance.

Continuing the Journey

Once you have caught a glimpse of the higher consciousness, you will know where the hidden treasure lies and, thereafter, can never be permanently dissuaded from your quest for the Truth, regardless of the interference, deterrents and great difficulties which must often be faced in this journey.

I then enrolled at New York University because the school offered courses that I believed would give me a better understanding of what I had experienced. I registered for classes entitled, "Unity and Diversity of Religion," "Psychology of Religion," and "Russian Occult."

At N.Y.U. I was introduced to many enlightening books and met many interesting people. I discovered others who had had mystical experiences similar to mine and were also traveling a path toward fulfillment.

I was attempting to understand the nature of my experiences. I was like one seeking the elephant by following its footprints when the elephant itself had been found.

All my life I was trying to please everyone but myself, because I believed that I was not worthy of their approval. The more I was driven the more I felt something was missing. I needed to prove to the world and to all of my father figures that I was not what they thought I was. Poverty of spirit needs external gratifications and I realized that when I did not receive the acceptance that I wished for, I would start another project, build another building, and acquire more worldly possessions that far surpassed those of my critics. But once I achieved and acquired my goals I was never truly satisfied.

After my enlightenment I felt at peace with myself for the first time in my life, and I came to the realization that all these cravings and desires were only veils of despair, and of no real value.

When I said I did not believe in God and spoke his name in vain, I was merely validating my unconscious belief in His existence. The more I assessed the situation, the more I strove to reverse the belief in others. The outcome brings the contradiction to perfection. By trying to prove that God did not exist, I proved to myself that God did exist.

I became aware that I was the one who was rejecting all that was good in me. All that was not well within me I projected onto others. This was the enemy within. Not until I accepted the love that existed within me that came from God, did I see and accept myself as I am now. I awakened out of the depth of my own nature and realized that nothing can bring man peace other than through his own efforts.

So long as the heart is troubled and disturbed by the excitement of desire, there is little chance that God will dwell therein. The beatific Godly vision occurs only in the heart which is calm and wrapped in divine communion.

As I had grown as a child in social consciousness, I now would be as a child and grow in spiritual consciousness. I was separated from my true center when I tried to follow the dictates of others rather than take responsibility for my own actions and do what I thought was right.

> This above all: to thine own self be true.
> And it must follow, as the night the day,
> Thou canst not then be false to any man.

William Shakespeare

This wisdom gave me the strength and peace that I was looking for. One must have the nature to trust everyone, but take responsibility for his own actions. The more enlightened we are, the more we discover the good and evil in man.

> When Banzan was walking through a market he overheard a conversation between a butcher and his customer.
> "Are all your meats fresh?" said the customer.
> "Everything in my shop is fresh," replied the

butcher. "You cannot find here any piece of meat that is not fresh."

At these words Banzan became enlightened.

This peace lasted for some time, but as time passed there came over me a sadness to see the world as it was, and not as it should be. The more I became aware of the sufferings of others, the more I suffered for and with them.

Purging

The man hath penance done.
And penance more will do.[2]

At this point in my life, when I was financially secure, I went into a business venture that put me in a very undesirable financial position. I called upon God for assistance and my consciousness asked, "Do I believe in God?" Because of my various experiences in the past, I said that I did.

A few days later I had a buyer for that business venture. I sold it on a land contract and told everyone that it was God that had interceded on my behalf.

As time passed, I began to doubt and question whether God really did intercede on my behalf, and my consciousness again asked, "Do I have faith in God?" I reluctantly said "Yes" and a few days later that transaction fell through.

Again Providence smiled on me and I leased a piece of property in which the income enhanced my financial position. I again told friends of mine with pride that God was taking very good care of me.

Just when I thought that my financial position was stable and everything was well with God and me, payments on a previous transaction ceased. I was very disappointed and my consciousness again asked, "Do I still believe in God and have faith in His guidance?" and again I reluctantly said, "Yes." I now wondered what the people whom I told that God had my best interest at heart were thinking when they could see that these transactions were going against my best interest, and everything seemed hopeless.

I later sold one of my businesses, subject to an option. Within six months I would receive payment in full and then all my financial problems would be resolved. Again I told people that I was being helped by divine providence. Within three months that deal fell through. I was now totally devastated, because I had been sure that this transaction would materialize and because I had made future commitments with the expectation of receiving this money.

I was beginning to question seriously my faith in God, and whether He was really working on my behalf. My consciousness indicated to me again that "I must believe." And after thinking about it for awhile I said, "I do believe." I was now becoming embarrassed in telling my friends that God had my best interest at heart and was looking after me.

After a short period of time the business I sold on an option which was not exercised became profitable. When I again felt that everything was well with God and myself, payments on the land I had leased, which enhanced my financial position, ceased because the anticipated financing fell through. Now all my investments were in serious jeopardy.

The contractor and the subcontractors began work on the project on the strength of the proposed financing and when it became evident that monies were not forthcoming, they halted construction and placed liens on all my properties. I was never in a more vulnerable financial position.

The developer was attempting to acquire financing from another bank in order to pay off all the liens from my property and complete the project. I did not feel that financing was likely, because of all the problems the banks and the savings and loans were having at the time.

I felt that the developer that leased my land could not fulfill his obligation and honor his commitment to the major tenant in time, so the major tenant would have "just cause" in backing out of his lease. This would put both the developer and me in a very undesirable financial position. I was now seriously doubting the existence of divine intervention.

Eventually the developer found another source of financing and a letter of commitment was issued subject to terms and conditions that were to be met by a certain date. I was very concerned as to whether both the major tenant and the financing commitment dates would or could be met. The final date to close the loan arrived and passed. The bank could now, at any time without notice, withdraw its binding commitment.

The person who leased my land and placed my assets in serious jeopardy related to me how he felt that he was being persecuted. Aware of the way he conducted business, I could see he was not about to take responsibility for his actions. For the first time in my life, I began to realize that I was being purged so that I would transcend my base finite conscious nature into infinite conscious awareness. Again that conscious awareness asked, "Is my faith strong enough?" And I answered, "Yes! I do believe." And this time I sincerely felt that God was within me, guiding me and helping me all along the way.

Finally the financing was acquired and construction had begun. The major tenant moved in and all was well, even though there may be many pitfalls to come.

Thro' many dangers, toil and snares,
I have already come;
'Tis grace that brought me safe this far,
And grace will lead me home.

The Lord has promised good to me,
His Word my hope secures,
He will my shield and portion be,
As long as life endures.

Yes, when this heart and flesh shall fall,
And mortal life shall cease,
I shall possess within the veil,
A life of Joy and peace.[12]

There are three factors that determine the result of
an action: human endeavor, time, and the wise working
of Divine Providence—the Goddess of Fate. The first
two factors are within one's control; it is the unknown
third factor that makes the difference between success
and failure.

> I said to the man who stood at the gate of the
> year; "Give me a light that I may tread safely
> into the unknown." And he replied; "Go out
> into the darkness and put thine hand into the
> hand of God. That shall be better than light
> and safer than a known way."

> M. Louise Haskins

God was within me, guiding me and helping me all
along the way. For what purpose? I now believe the
purpose was for my spiritual growth. I had now totally
accepted and surrendered to His will and guidance.

> But seek ye first the Kingdom of God and all
> his righteousness; and all these things shall
> be added unto you.
> Matthew 6:33

For a long while I used to circumambulate the Ka'bah. When I attained unto God, I saw the Ka'bah circumambulating me.

Bayzid al-Bistami

Beatific Vision

The direct conscious experience, eternally absorbed in the knowledge and love of God.

Most of my father's life was one of work and responsibilities. He came to America at the age of twelve with his father and his younger brother. His father returned to Greece and he never saw him or his mother again. One day late in his life he claimed that he saw them both come through the door while he was sitting in the kitchen. This was many years after their deaths.

They asked him how he was. He said he was fine and they asked him if he was ready to come with them. He said, "No," then they asked him if he would like to come with them. He again said, "No," and as they were leaving he heard them say that they would come back for him some other time.

This must have been a profound experience for my father, who doubted the existence of God, yet would faithfully go to church every Sunday. My father felt that if there was a God, there would not be all this pain and suffering. If he were God, he could do a far better job.

I always played the devil's advocate when my father and I discussed God and His creation. I remember one Sunday he asked me if I wanted to go to church with him and my mother. "What for?" was my answer. "For a man who does not believe in the existence of God, what purpose does it serve?"

After some verbal sparring he defended his position by saying he was doing it to please my mother. I proceeded to explain to him that was not the case because my mother had Alzheimer's disease and could not remember what day it was, let alone that it was Sunday.

He then left without me. I believe to this day that he went to church searching for something he was not able to put into words and searching for it in the institutional framework of the church.

My father had a stroke and spent the last days of his life in a nursing home. I had expected him at various times to pass away because of his suffering, but even the Angel of Death stands still and waits for a man with such a will.

The last time I visited my father I asked the nurse at the desk how he was. She told me that he was not well and was about to die.

I went into his room and he was lying there, looking like a ghost, all skin and bones, and staring at the ceiling. I hugged and kissed him and told him how much I loved him. I told him that the body was nothing but a machine. It had worn out and he must let it go.

I reminded him of the time his mother and father had come for him, and I told him that it was now time for him to go. He would soon be with his mother and father, as well as dwell in the heart of God; and when my time came, I would also join him in spirit. At that moment, I began to sing "Christ Has Arisen," a Greek Easter chant that my father would sing before supper at Easter time.

> Christ is Risen from the dead,
> By death trampling upon death.
> And to those in the tombs,
> Granting life eternal.

I do not know what compelled me to sing it again, but I did. When I had finished my father sat up just as the nurse was coming into the room. She took my father's vital signs and, to her surprise, found that they were all normal. She said that for four days his vital signs were dropping to the point that he was near death.

I gave him water and the nurse gave him grape juice to drink and then he laid back down. After the nurse left, I noticed that my father was smiling and at peace with himself. When I left he was still smiling.

> Destruction! What fury in your attack, how cruel your victory over this poor old body! You razed everything, you plunged a mind into abysses of anguish—and released the smile of ultimate joy.[5]

The next day when I returned my father was dead; his body was cold and like clay. My son was with me at the time, and I told him about the experience I had had with his grandfather the previous day. He told me to ask the nurse for a copy of the chart that they periodically recorded my father's vital signs on to see if he did experience something out of the ordinary.

To our surprise all of my father's vital signs prior to my coming were life threatening and when his vital signs were taken after I finished the chant "Christ has arisen," they were definitely normal.

It seemed to me that my father had found what he was searching for within himself; that which he was unable to find in the institutional framework of the church.

He must have experienced what some would call a beatific vision. Only this type of experience gives one the peace and serenity that I observed on his face that day.

Behold, I tell you a mystery: We shall not all sleep, but we shall all be changed,

In a moment, in the twinkling of an eye, at the last trumpet.

For the trumpet shall sound, and the dead shall be raised incorruptible, and we shall be changed.

For this corruptible must put on incorruption, and this mortal must put on immortality, then shall be brought to pass the saying that is written, Death is swallowed up in victory!

O death, where is thy sting? O grave, where is thy victory?

I Corinthians 15:51-55

Tozan went to see Nasen. At this time they were holding an anniversary meeting for Baso's death. Nansen said to the assembled monks, "We are going to celebrate Baso tomorrow. Do you think he will be present, or not?" No one among the monks answered; but Tozan said, "He will wait for a companion, and will come if he comes."

Who is the companion of an enlightened man? The answer clearly is God, but who is God? God is the expression of love. If you love Baso he will come and make his dwelling place with you. God shows Himself only to those who love Him in spirit and in truth.

Precious memories, unseen angels,
Sent from somewhere to my soul;
How they linger, ever near me,
And the sacred past unfold.

Precious father, loving mother,
Fly across the lonely years;
To old home scenes of my childhood,
With fond memories appear.

As I travel on life's pathway,
I know not what life shall hold;
As I wander hopes grow fonder,
Precious memories flood my soul.

Precious memories, how they linger,
How they ever flood my soul;
In the stillness of the midnight,
Precious, sacred scenes unfold.

Finite to Infinite Consciousness.
Mortality to Immortality

Observing such a change convinced me that there were two realities and that now my father's soul had passed over to an unknown realm, where we all must travel in the course of our journey through time and space.

Upon death the individual returns to the creative divinity which during life was reflected within his heart. This is not lost, but reabsorbed into the universe, from one conscious reality to another.

Could one be in both realities at the same time? Is it possible for a man to live in the field of action and yet, simultaneously, to live a life of eternal freedom in the blissful consciousness of absolute "Being?"

Is this what Jesus, Buddha, Krishna, Muhammad, and many other enlightened souls experienced, bringing that which is in heaven down here to earth? Acting with full interest in the world and yet living dialectically in the course of their finite earthly existence in ultimate God-consciousness? Is this what Buddha meant when he said,

> Before enlightenment one must chop wood
> and carry water and after enlightenment one
> must chop wood and carry water.

In this life one must not wish to die to be one with God, but to live to seek God and allow God to be one with him. To live in the world and to love the objects of the world, not for themselves alone, but for what there is in them of God. Not only do we gain the kingdom of love and peace after this life, but we may have it now. Eternity manifests itself in the consciousness of the here and now, and life at this moment is not a means to a future end, but is the end itself.

> The journey itself is home.   Basho

Continuing the Search

I went back to N.Y.U. and continued my studies and earned my Master's Degree in Religious Studies. After class one day a group of us went to a restaurant and discussed various subjects relating to religion. I told them about my profound experience at the ocean, where I had written the poem "Rebirth," four years earlier. I told them it was after this experience that I began to believe in the existence of God and His divine presence. Before then, I laughed in the face of God. After further discussion, I recited to them some of my earlier poems which were of a spiritual nature, including, "Immortality."

One of my fellow students then asked me when I had written "Immortality." I told her that it must have been more than fifteen years ago.

Validation

That night I had another profound dream. In the dream, I repeated what I had told the group at the restaurant that day. At the very moment I was asked when I had written the poem "Immortality," a Divine Presence informed me that "He" had been trying to reach me for many years, but I would not listen. I then woke up.

I now realize that in the past God showed me signs of His presence and His will, but I did not listen or pay heed. I also came to the realization that I and the Creator were indivisible, and that the essence of God has always been with me, guiding me from within, throughout my entire life.

> Lo I Am with you always. Even until the end of the earth.

Footprints

One night a man had a dream. He dreamed he was walking along the beach with the LORD. Across the sky flashed scenes from his life. For each scene, he noticed two sets of footprints in the sand; one belonging to him, and the other to the LORD.

When the last scene of his life flashed before him, he looked back at the footprints in the sand. He noticed that many times along the path of his life there was only one set of footprints. He also noticed that it happened at the very lowest and saddest times in his life.

This really bothered him and he questioned the LORD about it. "LORD, you said that once I decided to follow you, you'd walk with me all the way. But I have noticed that during the most troublesome times in my life, there is only one set of footprints. I don't understand why when I needed you most you would leave me."

The LORD replied, "My precious, precious child, I love you and I would never leave you. During your times of trial and suffering, when you see only one set of footprints, it was then that I carried you."

Author Unknown

Now that I have found thee, I know that in the first step I took, I moved away from thee.

When I was young, I despised and mocked the church, not realizing that what I resented was the institutional framework of the church, and not what it represented. Today I know it is a discipline, graceful and mystical, instrumental in reaching spiritual fulfillment. A human attempt to create a "divine" world here "on earth as it is in heaven." It has nothing to do with the dogmas that are presented to us over the years by self-seeking prophets. Theology deals tenderly with inward, beloved things, with grace and salvation.

Salvation is to be safe and happy in love and peace with all God's creation. The soul, when it is really at peace with itself, is at once united to God in love, truth and beauty. When man merges with the universal consciousness, he is liberated from the mundane illusions and delusions of the ordinary mind and the ego. Salvation is not an external event bestowed upon us, but an internal process of transformation. Salvation frees us from guilt of past sins but not from the obligation to repay its debt in kind. Only by overcoming guilt feelings can ego-consciousness realize its true nature and value.

When I heard the poem, "The Rime of the Ancient Mariner," I was deeply moved. For the first time, because of my experiences, I understood its depth and meaning.

> O Wedding-Guest! this soul hath been
> Alone on a wide wide sea;
> So lonely 'twas, that God himself
> Scarce seemed there to be.
>
> Farewell, farewell! but this I tell
> To thee, thou Wedding Guest!
> He prayeth well, who loveth well
> Both man and bird and beast.
>
> He prayeth best, who loveth best
> All things both great and small;
> For the dear God who loveth us,
> He made and loveth all.[2]

This was the answer I was looking for: the meaning and purpose of life. Unless we seek God and learn to see the light of God in every living creature, and unless we learn to love every living creature, we cannot say we love God. For God's light shines in all and the way back to God is through love.

Love thy neighbor as thyself   Galatians 5:14

It is the love and compassion towards ourselves that we project onto others. We should seek to love with a pure and sincere heart, so that we will know the love of God for all mankind; and, in so doing, know God's love as our own.

> Forthwith this frame of mine was wrenched
> With a woeful agony,
> Which forced me to begin my tale;
> And then it left me free.

Since then at an uncertain hour,
That agony returns:
And till my ghastly tale is told,
This heart within me burns.

I pass, like night, from land to land;
I have strange power of speech;
That moment that his face I see,
I know the man that must hear me:
To him my tale I teach.[2]

*

An old man going his lonely way,
Came at the evening cold and gray,
To a chasm, vast and deep and wide.
The old man crossed in the twilight dim,
The sullen stream had no fear for him.
But he turned when he got to the other side,
And built a bridge to span the tide.
"Good friend," said a fellow-pilgrim near,
"You're wasting your time while building here.
Your journey will end with the ending day,
You never again will pass this way.
Why build a bridge to span the tide?"
The traveler raised his old gray head,
"In the path I've come," he said,
"There followeth after me today
A fair haired youth who must pass this way.
This sullen stream which had no fear for me
May to this youth, a pitfall be.
He, too, must cross in the twilight dim,
Good friend, I'm building this bridge for him."

Author Unknown

POETRY

In loving memory of my mother for I remember sitting by her knees, looking up at her in awe listening to her read poetry when I was a little boy.

"Poetry is the Blossom and the fragrance of all human knowledge, human thoughts, human passions, emotion and language."

Samuel Taylor Coleridge

A PARADOX
"For Those Who See"

Games are played and games are fought,
Depending on the prize that's sought.
Played by rules from different books,
Some played by fools who do not look.

Ethics and morals are for ones such as we,
Winning without them would not give us glee.
The loss of respect for those so dear,
Will they lose our love, is what I fear.

An unfair advantage is taken by those,
Who grew up and confided in all our woes.
Reckless and ruthless wherever they go,
Knowing our weaknesses, they strike a hard blow.

The absence of God is all their reward,
For those who live and die by the sword.
In business or pleasure their goals should be,
Winning with love and respect for Thee.

It is difficult to accept and hard to understand,
To see it inflicted upon one's fellow man.
Is winning really winning from ones such as we?
An interesting paradox for those who see.

George A. Rapanos

IMMORTALITY
"Eternal Love"

We search when young, we search when old,
All search to find an intangible goal.
Thoughts of love and spirits bright
Bring joys and beauties of heaven in sight.

Feasts of silver and feasts of Gold,
Greed and envy hide the soul.
Toil and sweat, grief and pain,
Misery and hunger will not remain.

Time will come when all must die,
And find their soul at evening's tide.
With this spirit, the search will cease,
For this love is God, eternal peace.

George A. Rapanos

The Angel and the Peacock

There came to me in a dream so rare
A vision of love for an angel fair;
The glory of a peacock in days gone by,
So sad to see that time must fly.

Love's precious moments in the space of time
Must be appreciated like a glass of wine;
Enjoy your days with joy and bliss,
It may again be a time as this.

George A. Rapanos

Intertwined

Buds on flowers, leaves on trees,
Birds that sing to God and me;
To live and love all nature's kind,
Is to love oneself intertwined,

This love, this sweet ecstasy,
Brings the spirit closer to thee;
Encompassing wisdom, one will see
Our creator, a spirit, immortality.

George A. Rapanos

Spirituality

All around are dualities of life,
All around are Yin Yang of strife,
The spirit lies within.

George Rapanos

*

Spirituality

All around are the dualities of life,
All around are the Yin Yang of strife,
All polarities are the way of life,
The spirit lies within.

George Rapanos

REBIRTH
Enlightenment
An Elevated State of Consciousness

A Full—majestic moon—
   Radiates a beauty,
Over the vast turbulent sea.
   A veil is lifted!—A soul is free!—
To walk—the beach in radiant light.
   A spirit that blows across the water,
Stirring up the waves as—
   A heart is stirred by the thoughts of love,
Moving the ocean—to the shore—
   With waves that pulsate a desire to be—
Sea oats—in the sand dunes of time.
   Swaying—Reaching—
For the warmth of the Sun,
   A longing to procreate,
A reunion with————————GOD—

George Rapanos
June 1984

Revelation

Deep within the abyss, one's self encounter sees,
Radiant peace, a virgin spirit, tranquility.
Peace that lies beyond the presence of mind,
A spirit immortal, absence of time.

Trust in truth, yourself to bear,
Flower the path, that leads you there,
Tranquil with love, divine and serene,
Discover yourself, a spiritual being.

The mind a vision, a reflection sees,
That which is a sense of reality.
Pride, hate, anger, vengeance, and greed,
Repent! All are forms of iniquity.

Reality that surrounds us does not exist,
All are illusions, difficult to resist.
Lift up the veil, so the blind may see,
Judgments, deceptions and jealousies.

Peace, awareness, love of the soul,
Relinquish desires, experience the whole,
A witness to love, at peace are we,
All are one, that are one with thee......

George Rapanos
November 1984

Light and Beauty

Experience your Being, with the Divine,
Live within nature, intertwined.
Walk the earth, soar heavens above,
In light and beauty, expressions of Love.

George Rapanos
June 1985

THE HIDDEN TREASURE
"The Pearl of Great Worth"

There is a hidden Treasure,
Most search for it in vain.
It comes down from heaven,
And it falls like the rain.

This treasure is not one of silver,
This treasure is not one of gold.
The source of this hidden treasure,
Lies deep within one's soul.

A treasure more precious than silver,
A treasure more precious than gold.
To find this hidden treasure,
You must look within your soul.

George Rapanos
May 1989

A Heart Full of Love

There is a presence that guides us
A mystical presence indeed,
Beyond the rainbow's horizon,
That will guide us to be free.

Free from all fear and sorrow,
Free to be and to walk alone,
With eyes fixed to the heavens,
And a heart close to home.

Have faith in God's presence,
And you will walk with Him above.
You will find the hidden treasure,
When your heart is full of love.

George Rapanos
May 1989

Beyond the Horizon

The mind is forever yearning,
In this world of turmoil and strife.
Those who see beyond the horizon,
Are aware of eternal life.

George Rapanos

The Pilgrim's Journey

Come, come whoever you are,
Come from near or come from afar.
Sinner or saint in the end 'tis the same,
When one finds love and glorifies His name.

Come with music, a celebration to be,
Dancing forever in a state of ecstasy.
There is no darkness for those who flee,
All worldly treasures of iniquity.

Tonight, tonight the light does shine,
Giving birth to love in this heart of mine.
The music from heaven is all that I hear,
My heart is in love, I have nothing to fear.

When in love this soul does burn,
A fire, a vision, the lover yearns.
To see the world in your embrace,
Filled with love, filled with grace.

United in ecstasy we shall go,
No longer separated, no more woe.
Close your eyes and be with Him,
A hidden treasure that lies within.

George Rapanos
March 1990

Seeking God

Lord, where shall I find you,
Is Heaven your place?
Lord, where shall I find you?
I yearn for your Grace.

I sought you in heaven,
I sought you on earth.
I found you in heaven,
To earth you gave birth.

George Rapanos
March 1990

A Gift from God

On whose command was this world made,
Its cornerstone by whom was it laid?
Who made the mold wherein the world was cast,
With its truth and beauty, wide and vast?

Where stands the pillar on which it stands?
It's beyond all reason to understand.
God's truth and beauty are gifts from above
Follow your heart and leave the rest to love.

George Rapanos
October 1990

A Precious Gift

A Gift is not a gift,
Unless it is received;
Blessings of God's grace,
Are here for all to see.

Accept God's precious gift,
And pass it on with love;
To all who will receive it,
A gift from Heaven above.

George Rapanos
November 1992

A Phantom of Delight

She is a phantom of delight,
In thoughts of angelic light.
A mortal be, to share with me,
My deepest thoughts of eternity.

George Rapanos

Rose from Above

Come share an inspiring rose with me,
In a Spirit of mutual respect for thee.
Out of our chaos comes a rose from above,
In the Spirit of hope, In the Spirit of love.
To share our souls and let it be,
A rose from above, Immortality.

George Rapanos

THE PILGRIM'S QUEST

Rise up, Oh Phoenix of old,
Once again the story is told.
Out of the ashes of iniquity,
Rises the spirit of antiquity.

Play again love's ancient song,
That moves this searching pilgrim on.
A traveler in search of one's true goal,
Must seek the inner chamber of his soul.

Words of reason cannot express,
This love that suffers in my breast.
Longing for heaven here on earth,
Love and solitude gives it birth.

Fear and love must be set free,
Your spirit then will come to me.
This precious pearl of antiquity,
Will be my strength, my destiny.

No value is this precious pearl,
To greedy merchants of this world.
Give this love to the pilgrim's quest,
Where he will find peace and rest.

Uplift my heart and set me free,
A sweet fragrance of your majesty.
With love like a mother's care,
Thou shalt find thy image there.

Thou art the flowers in the spring,
Blooming in glory, your majesty sings.
Full of the joys and the glories of life,
Disturbed only by the winds of strife.

Let me rest this heart of mine,
Before I begin a task divine.
Cast aside this mortal shield,
Glories in heaven, to thee I yield.

Conceived in heaven on earth to dwell,
Forever creating a heaven or hell.
Time was spent in pride and sin,
Keeping away the prize to win.

The devil comes and is no more,
Leaving by the selfsame door.
Comes with fruits of pain and sin,
Leaves only by the way he was let in.

Let this pilgrim's vessel hide,
One's earthly mortal finite pride.
Fruits of his labor he must keep,
What he sows is what he reaps.

In this world of pain and care,
It is I alone, must my burden bear.
Lift the veil that is set between,
Reality and that which is a dream.

A handful of dust is all I own,
What matters is what I've sown.
On this branch of wisdom's tree,
Not a thorn will rise from me.

Deep in my heart a secret lies,
The sweetest song that yearns to rise.
From out of this gilded cage I sing,
The freedom bell, that longs to ring.

Mortals all, trapped are we,
In this vast world of iniquity.
Live your life so you may see,
The self, in all its treacheries.

Within the self the idol I,
Must be shattered, It must die.
Transform the self, you will see,
An angel from heaven, eternity.

This love that rises in me is divine,
Free of this world of space and time.
Ten thousand mysteries, one can see,
In one brief moment, all of eternity.

No pilgrim knows on his pilgrim's way,
If he be the hunter or the hunted prey.
What sets this pilgrim's world apart,
Is the faith of a pure and simple heart.

This pain that lies within my breast,
Longs for love to give it rest.
Cleanse my heart and lay it bare,
Thou shalt find Thy image there.

Seeking, on the road we trod,
To dwell within the heart of God.
Like us, he is seeking too,
To be our guardian of eternal rule.

God's presence is in all that is divine,
Our life, our soul is intertwined.
Seek Him now, you must depart
From the intellect to the heart.

Your love and grace have set me free,
From this world of passion, I want to be
Embraced in love, both night and day,
For on my knees, to Thee I pray.

Knowledge, Wisdom follow one by one,
Grasp this insight that you may come.
Know yourself in both heart and soul,
Within this journey is the pilgrim's goal.

What value is there in paper and pen,
If you fail to see that God is among men?
His image, his shadow is seen by all,
But many in number before him fall.

A handful of clay is my stock and trade,
Earthly treasures will all pass away.
Experience God's presence this very day,
For when life is over the body decays.

My heart declares a love for Thee,
In total submission you belong to me.
Receive these blessings and my grace,
And you will be lost in my embrace.

Those who have looked on the face of God,
Will travel with Him on the road we trod.
We have no knowledge when our time will come,
Prepare yourself before life is done.

We long and we search this wide world over,
We play in the mud and in the fields of clover.
Whether young or old we must all depart,
Better to leave this world with a joyful heart.

Armies marched in a cloud of dust,
Like tin soldiers they turned to rust.
Hear me now, my dearest of friends,
Before it's too late, life comes to an end.

This mortal form inevitably dies,
All are illusions, before our eyes.
Oh, dear God, If you would but see,
And fill my cup with your majesty.

Build me a bridge for I am but lost,
With stars of glory, that I may cross.
Be with me always, let me not despair,
In my footprints, I know you're there.

Give me the strength each time I pray,
To do your bidding, I will not stray.
To walk in your path is the pilgrim's way,
From sunrise to sunset, to the close of day.

Perceive that God and man are one,
Not unlike the rays of the golden sun.
Into this world I am bid to dwell,
To experience both its heaven or hell.

Sacred books are but letters and words,
Penetrate their meaning; they're not absurd.
Written with the mighty pen of love,
The message is one that comes from above.

What would I do with earth and sky,
If His grace and majesty pass me by?
Those who suffer, are in need of care,
God in His presence will be there.

Let me be like a bell that rings,
A joy to heaven, an angel sings.
To see Thy radiant presence of face,
To be lost forever in your embrace.

An atheist is one who does not see,
In his darkness your glorious majesty.
A heart that is cold and is like stone,
Will not sit on your Kingdom's throne.

I've lost my senses, but I am not mad,
Love has not forsaken me, if so 'tis sad.
Now and then like the wind it blows,
Now it comes and now it goes.

Hold my hand and lift me up,
To drink again from the golden cup.
Grasp my heart and set me free,
Sweet fragrance of your majesty.

Who knows my plight will understand,
What love will do from land to land.
I search for love and madly scream,
Is this dream a truth or this truth a dream?

Now hear this, lovers, and dear friends,
All that is on earth will come to an end.
Our lives will come and then be gone,
Like the wind that blows, passes on.

Why and how long will you keep from me,
Your spiritual presence that will set me free?
Its days and nights are all too brief,
With tears of sorrow and tears of grief.

A heart on fire, the lovers yearn,
For his soul in God, forever burns.
God's mighty love, within His breast,
Will take me home and give me rest.

The river of love will never run dry,
It fills your cup from heaven on high.
Where did it come from, this you ask,
To follow it back must be your task.

To be love's slave is not a curse,
It fills you with joy, a bountiful purse.
Love serves as a guide to the very end,
Back home again to a long-lost Friend.

So fill my cup and let me drink it dry,
In this space of time before I die.
Love is precious even here on earth,
Down from heaven that gave it birth.

Hear this, lovers, and dear friends,
Love is the messenger that heaven sends.
Spoken to many but heard by few,
Depends on perception, awareness and view.

You robbed me of anger, I want you to know,
With wisdom and insight, I will not let you go.
The truth is with me for the rest of my life,
Worldly affairs are nothing but strife.

I climbed the mountaintop to see,
A weaver weaving a home for me.
Heaven waits for us one and all,
Those most fortunate to hear the call.

My heart is burning with fire and pain,
Will my effort be rewarded or lost in vain?
With a heart full of love, a captive am I,
In this world of suffering until I die.

The angel of death waits at my door,
From heaven to earth and back once more.
All the secrets have been disclosed today,
I found my soul when I did not stray.

With this cup of love in hand,
I see again a long-lost Friend.
I'll make the choice, you be my guide,
For we shall travel, side by side.

Look not behind, nor look ahead,
For this is where fear will tread.
Before the news of death arrives,
Loose your self and the ego dies.

Let go of doctrines and any creed,
Grasp this message, it will set you free.
This is the breakthrough, no mortal will know,
To be one in God and with God to sow.

Days will come, the years will pass,
To be with God is our earthly task.
Once with God, you will know no pain,
Your life on earth will not be in vain.

Flesh is mortal and not the goal,
This body dies but not the soul.
Different paths that we must find,
To be with God, His grace divine.

Love and mercy rain down on me,
Cleanse my spirit, set me free.
Transcend the earth, both heaven and hell,
In silence be, no words can tell.

I call out to God, from mountains on high,
And soar with the birds into a heavenly sky.
God inspires, His nature is divine,
Transcend this world of space and time.

I am not here on earth for strife,
Love is the messenger and mission of life.
Be one with God and you will see,
The heavenly road that was meant to be.

Within the circumference the center I embrace,
To roam this world to experience His grace.
Grasping the secrets like one gone mad,
Detached from earthly pleasures I once had.

The fruits of my actions all will be,
The spirit of God that works through me.
Worldly pleasures fall one by one,
The treasures of heaven lay beyond the sun.

Perfect love is God's almighty plan,
As perfect as that of a grain of sand.
Our journey on earth will come to an end,
Perfect is the message that He sends.

Lift up the veil of earth and see,
In one brief moment, all eternity.
This moment is One, in the illusions of life,
Penetrate this veil and avoid the strife.

Unseen Horizons

The land is old, but my eyes have never seen
  London on a spring morning, beautiful and green,
How can I understand something I do not know?
  How can I not take the chance to learn and grow?
I have only one life, and a whole world yet to see.
  The mind is curiosity, there's a mountain somewhere for me.
I'll climb to the top and look out upon the sea;
  I'll discover why I was created, why I'm meant to be.
Everywhere I go and everything I do
  My mind will open to a life completely new.

                    Ruth E Rapanos
                    1985

LIFE

  Life is but time and space
  And means nothing until it's placed
  Into the hearts of those you love
  Which is cherished like a dove.

                    Ruth E Rapanos

A spirit that blows across the water,
stirring up the waves as —
A heart is stirred by the thoughts of love.

Favorite Poems

Olive Branch

How calmly does the olive branch,
observe the sky, begin to blanch.
Without a cry, without a prayer,
with no betrayal of despair.
Sometime, while the night observes the tree,
the zenith of its life will be
gone past forever, and from thence,
a second history will commence.
A chronicle, no longer gold,
a bargaining with mist and mold.
And finally the broken stem,
the plummeting to earth and then,
an intercourse, not well designed
for beings of a golden kind,
whose native dream must arch above
the earth's obscene corrupting love.
And still the ripe fruit and the branch,
observe the sky, begin to blanch.
Without a cry, without a prayer,
with no betrayal of despair.
Oh! courage, could you not as well
select a second place to dwell.
Not only in that golden tree,
but in the frightened heart of me.

Tennessee Williams

To Althea from Prison (excerpt)

Stone Walls do not a Prison make,
    Nor Iron Bars a Cage;
Minds innocent and quiet take
    That for an Hermitage;

If I have freedom in my Love,
    And in my soul am free;
Angels alone that soar above,
    Enjoy such liberty.

Richard Lovelace

The Daffodils

For oft, when on my couch I lie
In vacant or in pensive mood,
They flash upon the inward eye
Which is the bliss of solitude:
And then my heart with pleasure fills,
And dances with the daffodils.

Wordsworth

AD FINEM

On the white throat of the useless passion
    That scorched my soul with its burning breath
I clutched my fingers in murderous fashion,
    And gathered them close in a grip of death;
For why should I fan, or feed with fuel,
    A love that showed me but bland despair?
So my hold was firm, and my grasp was cruel—
    I meant to strangle it then and there!

I thought it was dead. But with no warning,
    It rose from its grave last night, and came
And stood by my bed till the early morning,
    And over and over it spoke your name.
Its throat was red where my hands had held it;
    It burned my brow with its scorching breath;
And I said, the moment my eyes beheld it,
    "A love like this can know no death."

For just one kiss that your lips have given
    In the lost and beautiful past to me,
I would gladly barter my hopes of Heaven
    And all the bliss of Eternity.
For never a joy are the angels keeping,
    To lay at my feet in Paradise,
Like that of into your strong arms creeping,
    And looking into your love-lit eyes.

I know, in the way that sins are reckoned,
    This thought is a sin of the deepest dye;
But I know, too, if an angel beckoned,
    Standing close by the Throne on High,
And you, adown by the gates infernal,
    Should open your loving arms and smile,
I would turn my back on things supernal,
    To lie on your breast a little while.

To know for an hour you were mine completely—
    Mine in body and soul, my own—
I would bear unending tortures sweetly,
    With not a murmur and not a moan.
A lighter sin or a lesser error
    Might change through hope or fear divine;
But there is no fear, and hell has no terror,
    To change or alter a love like mine.

                              Ella Wheeler Wilcox

A Psalm of Life

Tell me not, in mournful numbers,
    Life is but an empty dream!
For the soul is dead that slumbers,
    And things are not what they seem.

Life is real! Life is earnest!
    And the grave is not its goal;
Dust thou art, to dust returnest,
    Was not spoken of the soul.

Not enjoyment, and not sorrow,
    Is our destined end or way;
But to act, that each tomorrow
    Find us farther than today.

Art is long, and Time is fleeting,
    And our hearts, though stout and brave,
Still, like muffled drums, are beating
    Funeral marches to the grave.

In the world's broad field of battle,
    In the bivouac of life,
Be not like dumb, driven cattle!
    Be a hero in the strife!

Trust no Future, howe'er pleasant!
    Let the dead Past bury its dead!
Act,—act in the living Present!
    Heart within, and God o'erhead!

Lives of great men all remind us
    We can make our lives sublime,
And, departing, leave behind us
    Footprints on the sands of time.

Footprints, that perhaps another,
Sailing o'er life's solemn main,
A forlorn and shipwrecked brother,
Seeing, shall take heart again.

Let us then be up and doing,
With a heart for any fate;
Still achieving, still pursuing,
Learn to labor and to wait.

Henry Wadsworth
Longfellow

Sonnet 116

When in disgrace with fortune and men's eyes,
I all alone beweep my outcast state,
And trouble deaf Heaven with my bootless cries,
And look upon myself, and curse my fate,
Wishing me like to one more rich in hope,
Featur'd like him, like him with friends possess'd,
Desiring this man's art, and that man's scope,
With what I most enjoy contented least;
Yet in these thoughts myself almost despising
Haply I think on thee,—and then my state,
(Like to the lark at break of day arising)
From sullen earth sings hymns at heaven's gate;
  For thy sweet love remember'd such wealth brings,
  That then I scorn to change my state with kings.

William Shakespeare

Sonnet 29

Let me not to the marriage of true minds
Admit impediments; Love is not love
Which alters when it alteration finds,
Or bends with the remover to remove:
Oh, no! it is an ever-fixed mark,
That looks on tempests, and is never shaken;
It is the star to every wandering bark,
Whose worth's unknown, although his height be taken.
Love's not Time's fool, though rosy lips and cheeks
Within his bending sickle's compass come;
Love alters not with his brief hours and weeks,
But bears it out even to the edge of doom.
  If this be error, and upon me prov'd
  I never writ, nor no man ever lov'd.

William Shakespeare

New Friends and Old Friends

Make new friends, but keep the old;
Those are silver, these are gold.
New-made friendships, like new wine,
Age will mellow and refine.

Friendships that have stood the test—
Time and change—are surely best;
Brow may wrinkle, hair grow gray,
Friendship never knows decay.

For 'mid old friends, tried and true,
Once more we our youth renew.
But old friends, alas! may die;
New friends must their place supply.

Cherish friendship in your breast—
New is good, but old is best;
Make new friends, but keep the old;
Those are silver, these are gold.

Joseph Parry

The Day Is Done

The day is done, and the darkness
    Falls from the wings of Night,
As a feather is wafted downward
    From an eagle in his flight.

I see the lights of the village
    Gleam through the rain and the mist,
And a feeling of sadness comes o'er me
    That my soul cannot resist:

A feeling of sadness and longing,
    That is not akin to pain,
And resembles sorrow only
    As the mist resembles the rain.

Come, read to me some poem,
    Some simple and heartfelt lay,
That shall soothe this restless feeling,
    And banish the thoughts of day.

Not from the grand old masters,
    Not from the bards sublime,
Whose distant footsteps echo
    Through the corridors of Time.

For, like strains of martial music,
    Their mighty thoughts suggest
Life's endless toil and endeavor;
    And tonight I long for rest.

Read from some humbler poet,
    Whose songs gushed from his heart,
As showers from the clouds of summer,
    Or tears from the eyelids start;

Who, through long days of labor,
    And nights devoid of ease,
Still heard in his soul the music
    Of wonderful melodies.

Such songs have power to quiet
    The restless pulse of care,
And come like the benediction
    That follows after prayer.

Then read from the treasured volume
    The poem of thy choice,
And lend to the rhyme of the poet
    The beauty of thy voice.

And the night shall be filled with music
    And the cares, that infest the day,
Shall fold their tents, like the Arabs,
    And as silently steal away.

                    Henry Wadsworth
                    Longfellow

Thanatopsis

To him who, in the love of Nature, holds
Communion with her visible forms, she speaks
A various language; for his gayer hours
She has a voice of gladness, and a smile
And eloquence of beauty; and she glides
Into his darker musings, with a mild
And healing sympathy, that steals away
Their sharpness, ere he is aware. When thoughts
Of the last bitter hour come like a blight
Over thy spirit, and sad images
Of the stern agony, and shroud, and pall,
And breathless darkness, and the narrow house,
Make thee to shudder, and grow sick at heart,—
Go forth under the open sky, and list
To Nature's teachings, while from all around—
Earth and her waters, and the depths of air—
Comes a still voice:—Yet a few days, and thee
The all-beholding sun shall see no more
In all his course; nor yet in the cold ground,
Where thy pale form was laid, with many tears,
Nor in the embrace of ocean, shall exist
Thy image, Earth, that nourished thee, shall claim
Thy growth, to be resolved to earth again;
And, lost each human trace, surrendering up
Thine individual being, shalt thou go
To mix forever with the elements;
To be a brother to the insensible rock,
And to the sluggish clod, which the rude swain
Turns with his share, and treads upon. The oak
Shall send his roots abroad, and pierce thy mold.

Yet not to thine eternal resting place
Shalt thou retire alone—nor couldst thou wish
Couch more magnificent. Thou shalt lie down
With patriarchs of the infant world—with kings,

The powerful of the earth—the wise, the good,
Fair forms, and hoary seers of ages past,
All in one mighty sepulcher. The hills,
Rock-ribbed, and ancient as the sun; the vales
Stretching in pensive quietness between;
The venerable woods—rivers that move
In majesty, and the complaining brooks,
That make the meadows green; and poured round all
Old ocean's gray and melancholy waste—
Are but the solemn decorations all
Of the great tomb of man! The golden sun,
The planets, all the infinite host of heaven,
Are shining on the sad abodes of death,
Through the still lapse of ages. All that tread
The globe are but a handful to the tribes
That slumber in its bosom.—Take the wings
Of morning, pierce the Barcan wilderness,
Or lose thyself in the continuous woods
Where rolls the Oregon and hears no sound
Save his own dashings—yet the dead are there;
And millions in those solitudes, since first
The flight of years began, have laid them down
In their last sleep—the dead reign there alone!

    So shalt thou rest,—and what if thou withdraw
In silence from the living; and no friend
Take note of thy departure? All that breathe
Will share thy destiny. The gay will laugh
When thou art gone, the solemn brood of care
Plod on, and each one as before shall chase
His favorite phantom; yet all these shall leave
Their mirth and their employments, and shall come
And make their bed with thee. As the long train
Of ages glides away, the sons of men—
The youth in life's green spring, and he who goes

In the full strength of Years, matron and maid,
And the sweet babe, and the gray-headed man,—
Shall one by one be gathered to thy side,
By those, who in their turn shall follow them.

  So live that when thy summons comes to join
The innumerable caravan, that moves
To that mysterious realm, where each shall take
His chamber in the silent halls of death,
Thou go not, like the quarry-slave at night,
Scourged to his dungeon, but, sustained and soothed
By an unfaltering trust, approach thy grave,
Like one who wraps the drapering of his couch
About him, and lies down to pleasant dreams.

William Cullen Bryant

How the Great Guest Came

BEFORE THE CATHEDRAL in grandeur rose,
At Ingelburg where the Danube goes;
Before its forest of silver spires
Went airily up to the clouds and fires;
Before the oak had ready a beam,
While yet the arch was stone and dream—
There where the altar was later laid,
Conrad, the cobbler, plied his trade.

* * *

It happened one day at the year's white end—
Two neighbors called on their old-time friend;
And they found the shop, so meager and mean,
Made gay with a hundred boughs of green.
Conrad was stitching with face ashine,
But suddenly stopped as he twitched a twine:
"Old friends, good news! At dawn today,
As the cocks were scaring the night away,
The Lord appeared in a dream to me,
And said, 'I am coming your Guest to be!'
So I've been busy with feet astir,
Strewing the floor with branches of fir.
The wall is washed and the shelf is shined,
And over the rafter the holly twined.
He comes today, and the table is spread
With milk and honey and wheaten bread."

His friends went home; and his face grew still
As he watched for the shadow across the still.
He lived all the moments o'er and o'er,
When the Lord should enter the lowly door—
The knock, the call, the latch pulled up,
The lighted face, the offered cup.
He would wash the feet where the spikes had been,
He would kiss the hands where the nails went in,

And then at the last would sit with Him
And break the bread as the day grew dim.

While the cobbler mused there passed his pane
A beggar drenched by the driving rain.
He called him in from the stony street
And gave him shoes for his bruised feet.
The beggar went and there came a crone,
Her face with wrinkles of sorrow sown.
A bundle of fagots bowed her back,
And she was spent with the wrench and rack.
He gave her his loaf and steadied her load
As she took her way on the weary road.
Then to his door came a little child,
Lost and afraid in the world so wild,
In the big, dark world. Catching it up,
He gave it the milk in the waiting cup,
And led it home to its mother's arms,
Out of the reach of the world's alarms.

The day went down in the crimson west
And with it the hope of the blessed Guest,
And Conrad sighed as the world turned gray:
"Why is it, Lord, that your feet delay?"
Did You forget that this was the day?"
Then soft in the silence a Voice he heard:
"Lift up your heart, for I kept my word.
Three times I came to your friendly door;
Three times my shadow was on your floor.
I was the begger with bruised feet;
I was the woman you gave to eat;
I was the child on the homeless street!"

Edwin Markham

The Rhodora

On Being Asked Whence Is the Flower

In May, when sea-winds pierced our solitudes,
I found the fresh Rhodora in the woods,
Spreading its leafless blooms in a damp nook,
The purple petals, fallen in the pool,
Made the black water with their beauty gay;
Here might the redbird come his plumes to cool,
And court the flower that cheapens his array.
Rhodora! if the sages ask thee why
This charm is wasted on the earth and sky,
Tell them, dear, that if eyes were made for seeing
Then Beauty is its own excuse for being:
Why thou wert there, O rival of the rose!
I never thought to ask, I never knew:
But, in my simple ignorance, suppose
The self-same Power that brought me there brought you.

Ralph Waldo Emerson

Renascence

All I could see from where I stood
Was three long mountains and a wood;
I turned and looked another way,
And saw three islands in a bay.
So with my eyes I traced the line
Of the horizon, thin and fine,
Straight around till I was come
Back to where I'd started from;
And all I saw from where I stood
Was three long mountains and a wood.
Over these things I could not see;
These were the things that bounded me;
And I could touch them with my hand,
Almost, I thought, from where I stand.
And all at once things seemed so small
My breath came short, and scarce at all.
But, sure, the sky is big, I said;
Miles and miles above my head;
So here upon my back I'll lie
And look my fill into the sky.
And so I looked, and, after all,
The sky, was not so very tall.
The sky, I said, must somewhere stop,
And—sure enough!—I see the top!
The sky, I thought, is not so grand;
I most could touch it with my hand!
And, reaching up my hand to try,
I screamed to feel it touch the sky.
I screamed, and—lo!—Infinity
Came down and settled over me;
Forced back my scream into my chest,
Bent back my arm upon my breast,
And, pressing of the Undefined
The definition on my mind,

Held up before my eyes a glass
Through which my shrinking sight did pass
Until it seemed I must behold
Immensity made manifold;
Whispered to me a word whose sound
Deafened the air for worlds around,
And brought unmuffled to my ears
The gossiping of friendly spheres,
The creaking of the tented sky,
The ticking of Eternity.

I saw and heard, and knew at last
The How and Why of all things, past,
And present, and forevermore.
The universe, cleft to the core,
Lay open to my probing sense
That, sickening, I would fain pluck thence
But could not,—nay! But needs must suck
At the great wound, and could not pluck
My lips away till I had drawn
All venom out.—Ah, fearful pawn!
For my omniscience I paid toll
In infinite remorse of soul.
All sin was of my sinning, all
Atoning mine, and mine the gall
Of all regret. Mine was the weight
Of every brooded wrong, the hate
That stood behind each envious thrust,
Mine every greed, mine every lust.
And all the while for every grief,
Each suffering, I craved relief
With individual desire,—
Craved all in vain! And felt fierce fire
About a thousand people crawl;
Perished with each,—then mourned for all!

A man was starving in Capri;
He moved his eyes and looked at me;
I felt his gaze, I heard his moan,
And knew his hunger as my own.
I saw at sea a great fog-bank
Between two ships that struck and sank;
A thousand screams the heavens smote;
And every scream tore through my throat;
No hurt I did not feel, no death
That was not mine; mine each last breath
That, crying, met an answering cry
From the compassion that was I.
All suffering mine, and mine its rod;
Mine, pity like the pity of God.
Ah, awful weight! Infinity
Pressed down upon the finite me!
My anguished spirit, like a bird,
Beating against my lips I heard;
Yet lay the weight so close about
There was no room for it without.
And so beneath the weight lay I
And suffered death, but could not die.

Long had I lain thus, craving death,
When quietly the earth beneath
Gave way, and inch by inch, so great
At last had grown the crushing weight,
Into the earth I sank till I
Full six feet under ground did lie,
And sank no more,—there is no weight
Can follow here, however great.
From off my breast I felt it roll,
And as it went my tortured soul
Burst forth and fled in such a gust
That all about me swirled the dust.

Deep in the earth I rested now;
Cool is its hand upon the brow
And soft its breast beneath the head
Of one who is so gladly dead.
And all at once, and over all,
The pitying rain began to fall,
I lay and heard each pattering hoof
Upon my lowly, thatched roof.
And seemed to love the sound far more
Than ever I had done before.
For rain it hath a friendly sound
To one who's six feet underground;
And scarce the friendly voice of face:
A grave is such a quiet place.

The rain, I said, is kind to come
And speak to me in my new home.
I would I were alive again
To kiss the fingers of the rain,
To drink into my eyes the shine
Of every slanting silver line,
To catch the freshened, fragrant breeze
From drenched and dripping apple-trees.
For soon the shower will be done,
And then the broad face of the sun
Will laugh above the rain-soaked earth
Until the world with answering mirth
Shakes joyously, and each round drop
Rolls, twinkling, from its grass-blade top.
How can I bear it; buried here,
While overhead the sky grows clear
And blue again after the storm?
O, multi-colored, multiform,
Beloved beauty over me,
That I shall never, never see

Again! Spring-silver, autumn-gold,
That I shall never more behold!
Sleeping your myriad magic through,
Close-sepulchered away from you!
O God, I cried, give me new birth,
And put me back upon the earth!
Upset each cloud's gigantic gourd
And let the heavy rain, down-poured
In one big torrent, set me free,
Washing my grave away from me!

I ceased; and, through the breathless hush
That answered me, the far-off rush
Of herald wings came whispering
Like music down the vibrant string
Of my ascending prayer, and—crash!
Before the wild winds whistling lash
The startled storm-clouds reared on high
And plunged in terror down the sky,
And the big rain in one black wave
Fell from the sky and struck my grave.
I know not how such things can be;
I only know there came to me
A fragrance such as never clings
To aught save happy living things;
A sound as of some joyous elf
Singing sweet songs to please himself,
And through and over everything,
A sense of glad awakening.
The grass, a tip-toe at my ear,
Whispering to me I could hear;
I felt the rain's cool finger-tips
Brushed tenderly across my lips,
Laid gently on my sealed sight,
And all at once the heavy night

Fell from my eyes and I could see,—
A drenched and dripping apple-tree.
A last long line of silver rain,
A sky grown clear and blue again.
And as I looked a quickening gust
Of wind blew up to me and thrust
Into my face a miracle
Of orchard-breath, and with the smell,—
I know not how such things can be!—
I breathed my soul back into me.
Ah! Up then from the ground sprang I
And hailed the earth with such a cry
As is not heard save from a man
Who has been dead, and lives again.

About the trees my arms I wound;
Like one gone mad I hugged the ground;
I raised my quivering arms on high;
I laughed and laughed into the sky,
Till at my throat a strangling sob
Caught fiercely, and a great heart-throb
Sent instant tears into my eyes;
O God, I cried, no dark disguise
Can e'er hereafter hide from me
Thy radiant identity!
Thou canst not move across the grass
But my quick eyes will see Thee pass,
Nor speak, however silently,
But my hushed voice will answer Thee.
I know the path that tells Thy way
Through the cool eve of every day;
God, I can push the grass apart
And lay my finger on Thy heart!

The world stands out on either side
No wider than the heart is wide;

Above the world is stretched the sky,
No higher than the soul is high.
The heart can push the sea and land
Farther away on either hand;
The soul can split the sky in two,
And let the face of God shine through.
But East and West will pinch the heart
That cannot keep them pushed apart;
And he whose soul is flat—the sky
Will cave in on him by and by.

Edna St. Vincent Millay

Hamlet (excerpt)

I have of late,—but wherefore I know not,—lost all my mirth, foregone all custom of exercises; and, indeed it goes so heavily with my disposition that this goodly frame the earth, look you this, brave o'erhanging firmament, this majestical roof, fretted with golden fire,—why, it seems no other thing to me than a foul and pestilent congregation of vapours.

What a piece of work is man! How infinite in faculties! in form and moving, how express and admirable! in action, how like an angel! in movement, how like a god! the beauty of the world! the paragon of animals! And yet, to me, what is this quintessence of dust?

William Shakespeare

Hamlet (excerpt)

To be, or not to be: that is the question.
Whether 'tis nobler in the mind to suffer
The slings and arrows of outrageous fortune,
Or to take arms against a sea of troubles,
And by opposing end them? To die; to sleep;
No more; and by a sleep to say we end
The heart-ache and the thousand natural shocks
That flesh is heir to. 'Tis a consummation
Devoutly to be wish'd. To die; to sleep;
To sleep? Perchance to dream! Ay, there's the rub;

For in that sleep of death what dreams may come,
When we have shuffl'd off this mortal coil,
Must give us pause. There's the respect
That makes calamity of so long life.
For who would bear the whips and scorns of time,
The oppressor's wrong, the proud man's contumely,
The pangs of despriz'd love, the law's delay,
The insolence of office, and the spurns
That patient merit of the unworthy takes,
When he himself might his quietus make
With a bare bodkin? Who would fardels bear,
To grunt and sweat under a weary life,
But that the dread of something after death,
The undiscovered country, from whose bourn
No traveller returns, puzzles the will,
And makes us rather bear those ills we have
Then fly to others that we know not of?

William Shakespeare

The Conference of the Birds (excerpt)

Every pilgrim takes a different way,
And different spirits different rules obey.
There are so many roads and each is fit
For that one pilgrim who must follow it.
How could a spider or a tiny ant.
Tread the same path as some huge elephant:
Our pathways differ—no man ever knows
The secret route by which another goes.

Farid ud-Din Attar

Memory

MY CHILDHOOD'S HOME I see again,
    And sadden with the view;
And still, as memory crowds my brain,
    There's pleasure in it, too.

O memory! thou midway world
    'Twixt earth and paradise,
Where things decayed and loved ones lost
    In dreamy shadows rise,

And, freed from all that's earthly, vile,
    Seem hallowed, pure and bright,
Like scenes in some enchanted isle
    All bathed in liquid light.

As dusky mountains please the eye
    When twilight chases day;
As bugle notes that, passing by,
    In distance die away;

As, leaving some grand waterfall,
    We, lingering, list its roar—
So memory will hallow all
    We've known but know no more.

Near twenty years have passed away
    Since here I bid farewell
To woods and fields, and scenes of play,
    And playmates loved so well.

Where many were, but few remain
    Of old familiar things,
But seeing them to mind again
    The lost and absent brings.

The friends I left that parting day,
    How changed, as time has sped!
Young childhood grown, strong manhood gray;
    And half of all are dead.

I hear the loved survivors tell
    How nought from death could save,
Till every sound appears a knell
    And every spot a grave.

I range the fields with pensive tread,
    And pace the hollow rooms,
And feel (companion of the dead)
    I'm living in the tombs.

Abraham Lincoln

A Vanishing Friend

Around the corner I have a friend,
In this great city that has no end.
Yet days go by and weeks rush on,
And before I know it a year is gone.
And I never see my old friend's face,
For life is a swift and terrible race.
He knows I like him just as well
As in the days when I rang his bell
And he rang mine. We were younger then,
And now we are busy, tired men—
Tired with playing a foolish game,
Tired with trying to make a name.
"Tomorrow," I say, "I will call on Jim,
Just to show that I'm thinking of him."
But tomorrow comes and tomorrow goes,
And the distance between us grows and grows,
Around the corner—yet miles away—
"Here's a telegram, sir,"—"Jim died today."
And that's what we get, and deserve in the end—
Around the corner, a vanishing friend.

Author Unknown

The Touch of the Master's Hand

'Twas battered and scarred, and the auctioneer
Thought it scarcely worth its while
To waste much time on the old violin,
But held it up with a smile:
"What am I bidden, good folks," he cried,
"Who'll start the bidding for me?"
"A dollar, A dollar", then, "Two!" "Only two?
Two dollars and who'll make it three?
Three dollars, once; three dollars, twice;
Going for three—" But no,
From the room, far back, a gray-haired man,
Came forward and picked up the bow;
Then, wiping the dust from the old violin,
And tightening the loose strings,
He played a melody pure and sweet
As a caroling angel sings.

The music ceased, and the auctioneer,
With a voice that was quiet and low,
Said: "What am I bid for the old violin?"
And he held it up with the bow.
"A thousand dollars, and who'll make it two?
Two thousand! And who'll make it three?
Three thousand, once, three thousand, twice,
And going, and gone," said he.
The people cheered, but some of them cried,
"We do not quite understand
What changed its worth?" Swift came the reply:
"The touch of the Master's hand."

And many a man with life out of tune,
And battered and scarred with sin,
Is auctioned cheap to the thoughtless crowd,
Much like the old violin.

129

A "mess of pottage," a glass of wine;
A game—and he travels on.
He is "going" once, "going" twice,
He's "going" and almost "gone."
But the master comes, and the foolish crowd
Never can quite understand
The worth of a soul and the change that's wrought
By the touch of the Master's hand.

Myra Brooks Welch

A King Who Built a Splendid Palace

A king who loved his own magnificence
Once built a palace and spared no expense.
When this celestial building had been raised,
The gorgeous carpets and its splendour dazed
The crowd that pressed around—a servant flung
Trays heaped with money to the scrabbling throng.
The king now summoned all his wisest friends
And said: "What do I lack? Who recommends
Improvements to my court?" "We must agree,"
They said, "no man could now or ever see,
In all the earth, a palace built like this."
An old ascetic spoke. "One thing's amiss,"
He said; "there's one particular you lack.
This noble structure has a nasty crack
(Though if it weren't for that it would suffice
To be the heavenly court of paradise)."
The king replied: "What crack? Where is it? Where?
If you've come here for trouble, then take care!"
The man said: "Lord, it is the truth I tell—
And through that crack will enter Azra'el.*
It may be you can block it, but if not,
Then throne and palace are not worth a jot!
Your palace now seems like some heavenly prize,
But death will make it ugly to your eyes;
Nothing remains for ever and you know—
Don't pride yourself on things that cannot last;
Don't gallop your high-stepping horse so fast.
If one like me is left to indicate
Your faults to you, I pity your sad fate."

*The angel of death.

The Conference of the Birds
Farid ud-Din Attar

The Winds of Fate

One ship drives east and another drives west
  With the selfsame winds that blow.
    'Tis the set of the sails
    And not the gales
  Which tells us the way to go.

Like the wind of the sea are the ways of fate
  As we voyage along through life:
    'Tis the set of a soul
    That decides its goal,
  And not the calm or the strife.

Ella Wheeler Wilcox

The Prayer of the Cock

Do not forget, Lord,
it is I who makes the sun rise.
I am Your servant
but, with the dignity of my calling,
I need some glitter and ostentation.
Noblesse oblige....
All the same,
I am Your servant,
only... Do not forget, Lord,
I make the sun rise.

The Fool's Prayer

The royal feast was done; the King
Sought some new sport to banish care,
And to his jester cried; "Sir Fool,
Kneel now, and make for us a prayer!"

The jester doffed his cap and bells,
And stood the mocking court before;
They could not see the bitter smile
Behind the painted grin he wore.

He bowed his head, and bent his knee
Upon the monarch's silken stool;
His pleading voice arose: "O Lord,
Be merciful to me, a fool!

"No pity, Lord, could change the heart
From red with wrong to white as wool;
The rod must heal the sin: but, Lord,
Be merciful to me, a fool!

"'Tis not by guilt the onward sweep
Of truth and right, O Lord, we stay;
'Tis by our follies that so long
We hold the earth from heaven away.

"These clumsy feet, still in the mire,
Go crushing blossoms without end;
These hard, well-meaning hands we thrust
Among the heart-strings of a friend.

"The ill-timed truth we might have kept—
Who knows how sharp it pierced and stung?
The word we had not sense to say—
Who knows how grandly it had rung?

"Our faults no tenderness should ask,
The chastening stripes must cleanse them all;
But for our blunders—oh, in shame
Before the eyes of heaven we fall.

"Earth bears no balsam for mistakes;
Men crown the knave, and scourge the tool
That did his will; but Thou, O Lord,
Be merciful to me, a fool!"

The room was hushed, in silence rose
The King, and sought his gardens cool.
And walked apart, and murmured low,
"Be merciful to me, a fool!"

Edward R. Sill

He who knows he is a great fool, is not such a great fool.

Chung tsu

A Drunkard Accuses a Drunkard

A sot became extremely drunk—his legs
And head sank listless, weighed by wine's thick dregs.
A sober neighbour put him in a sack
And took him homewards hoisted on his back.
Another drunk went stumbling by the first,
Who woke and stuck his head outside and cursed.
"Hey, you, you lousy dipsomaniac,"
He yelled as he was borne off in the sack,
"If you'd had fewer drinks, just two or three,
You would be walking now as well as me."
He saw the other's state but not his own,
And in this blindness he is not alone;
You cannot love, and this is why you seek
To find men vicious, or depraved, or weak—
If you could search for love and persevere
The sins of other men would disappear.[1]

When I Was One and Twenty

When I was one and twenty,
I heard a wise man say,
"Give crowns, pounds, and guineas,
but not your heart away;

Give rubies away and pearls,
But keep your fancy free."
For I was one and twenty,
No use to talk to me.

When I was one and twenty,
I heard him say again,
"The heart out of the bosom,
Was never given in vain;

Tis paid with sighs aplenty,
And sold for endless rue."
And now I'm two and twenty,
Oh, "Tis true, tis true."

The Devout Slave

A negro had a slave devout and wise
Who at an early hour would wake and rise,
Then pray until the sun came peeping through.
His master said: "Wake me up early too,
And we can pray together till the dawn."
The slave said: "Just before a baby's born,
Who tells the mother, 'Now your time draws near'?
She knows it does—her pain has made it clear;
If you have felt this pain you are awake—
No other man can feel it for your sake.
If someone has to rouse you every day,
Then someone else instead of you should pray."
The man without this pain is not a man;
May grief destroy the bragging charlatan!
But one who is entangled in its spell
Forgets all thoughts of heaven or of hell.

The Devil Complains

A sluggard once approached a fasting saint
And, baffled by despair, made this complaint:
"The devil is a highwayman, a thief,
Who's ruined me and robbed me of belief."
The saint replied: "Young man, the devil too
Has made his way here to complain—of you.
'My province is the world,' I heard him say;
'Tell this new pilgrim of God's holy Way
To keep his hands off what is mine—if I
Attack him it's because his fingers pry
In my affairs; if he will leave me be,
He's no concern of mine and can go free.'"

The Conference of the Birds
Farid ud-Din Attar

Abou Ben Adhem

Abou Ben Adhem (may his tribe increase!)
Awoke one night from a deep dream of peace,
And saw, within the moonlight in his room,
Making it rich, and like a lily in bloom,
An Angel writing in a book of gold:
Exceeding peace had made Ben Adhem bold,
and to the Presence in the room he said,
"What writest thou?" The Vision raised its head,
And with a look made of all sweet accord
Answered, "The names of those who love the Lord."
"And is mine one?" said Abou. "Nay, not so,"
Replied the Angel. Abou spoke more low,
But cheerly still; and said, "I pray thee, then,
Write me as one that loves his fellow-men."

The Angel wrote, and vanished. The next night
It came again with a great wakening light,
And showed the names whom love of God had blessed,
And, lo! Ben Adhem's name led all the rest!

James Henry Leigh Hunt

Annabel Lee

IT WAS MANY and many a year ago,
    In the kingdom by the sea,
That a maiden there lived whom you may know
    By the name of Annabel Lee;
And this maiden she lived with no other thought
    Than to love and be loved by me.

I was a child and she was a child,
    In this kingdom by the sea;
But we loved with a love that was more than love,
    I and my Annabel Lee;
With a love that the winged seraphs of heaven
    Coveted her and me.

And this was the reason that, long ago,
    In this kingdom by the sea,
A wind blew out of a cloud, chilling
    My beautiful Annabel Lee;
So that her high-born kinsman came
    And bore her away from me,
To shut her up in a sepulcher
    In this kingdom by the sea.

The angels, not half so happy in heaven,
    Went envying her and me.
Yes, that was the reason—as all men know,
    In this kingdom by the sea—
That the wind came out of the cloud by night,
    Chilling and killing my Annabel Lee.

But our love it was stronger far than the love
　　Of those that were older than we,
　　Of many far wiser than we.
And neither the angels in heaven above,
Nor the demons down under the sea,
Can ever dissever my soul from the soul
　　Of the beautiful Annabel Lee:

For the moon never beams without bringing me
dreams
　　Of the beautiful Annabel Lee;
And the stars never rise but I feel the bright eyes
　　Of the beautiful Annabel Lee;
And so, all the night-tide, I lie down by the side
Of my darling, my darling, my life, and my bride,
　　In the sepulcher there by the sea,
　　In her tomb by the sounding sea.

　　　　　　　　　　Edgar Allan Poe

To My Old Yellow Dog

You were only a babe when you first came to me;
Just 'bout as small as a puppy could be;
And I wasn't much older, hardly two;
But my first childhood memories encompassed you.

You first learned to wobble and bark out loud.
You got into mischief that wasn't allowed.
When you were older, you helped drive the cow.
How well I remember my teaching you how!

You stepped on my marbles and knawed on my ball;
You dug in my garden and tracked in the hall.
How often I hunted—could not find my hat;
How often I'd yell to you "don't chase the cat."

Remember those hunting trips, oft dearly bought?
Remember the squirrels and the rabbits we caught?
Remember the bobwhite down by the track?
Whenever we'd call him—he'd answer us back!

In summer we went to the old swimming hole.
Remember the blue grass where you lay and rolled?
And when in the winter I'd go there to skate;
You could do nothing but stand there and wait.

Four-footed champion of a schoolboy's heart;
In whose sorrows and pleasures you played such a part.
Pal of my days when life was new!
I stand in reverence—now—to you.

From the day that father took you in;
A stranger in a world of men;
You were my playmate good as gold!
You knew all my secrets and never told!

The years never dealt you a world of strife.
The Grim Reaper took you—A victim of life!
Since you left me, I'm lonely—fate wasn't fair;
But I'll meet you in Heaven—Please wait for me there!

Hubert Russel Foster
16 years old, 1923

Annie and Willie's Prayer

"Twas the eve before Christmas. "Goodnight," had been said,
And Annie and Willie had crept into bed;
There were tears on their pillows, and tears in their eyes,
And each little bosom was heaving with sighs,
For tonight their stern father's command had been given
That they should retire precisely at seven
Instead of at eight—for they troubled him more
With questions unheard of than ever before.
He had told them he thought this delusion a sin,
No such thing as "Santa Claus" ever had been.
And he hoped, after this, he would never more hear
How he scrambled down chimneys with presents each year.
And this was the reason that two little heads
So restlessly tossed on their soft downy beds.
Eight, nine, and the clock in the steeple tolled ten,
Not a word had been spoken by either till then,
When Willie's sad face from the blanket did peep,
And whispered, "Dear Annie, is you fast asleep?"
"Why no, brother Willie," a sweet voice replied,
"I've tried in vain, but I can't shut my eyes,
For somehow it makes me so sorry because
Dear Papa has said there is no 'Santa Claus.'
Now we know there is, and it can't be denied,
For he came every year before mamma died;
"But then I've been thinking that she used to pray,
And God would hear everything mamma would say.
And maybe she asked him to send Santa Claus here
With that sackfull of presents he brought every year."
"Well, why tan't we p'ay dest as mamma did den,
And ask Dod to send him with p'esents aden?"
"I've been thinking so, too," and without a word more,
Four little bare feet bounded out on the floor,
And four little knees the soft carpet pressed,
And two tiny hands were clasped close to each breast.

"Now, Willie, you know we must firmly believe
That the presents we ask for we're sure to receive;
You must wait very still till I say the 'amen,'
And by that you will know that your turn has come then."

"Dear Jesus, look down on my brother and me,
And grant us the favor we are asking of Thee.
I want a wax dolly, a teaset and ring,
And an ebony workbox that shuts with a spring.
Bless papa, dear Jesus, and cause him to see
That Santa Claus loves us as much as does he;
Don't let him get fretful and angry again
At dear brother Willie and Annie. Amen."
"Pease, Desus, 'et Santa Taus tum down tonight,
And b'ing us some p'esents before it is light.
I want he should div' me a nice 'ittie s'ed,
With b'ite shinin' 'unners, and all painted red;
A box full of tandy, a book and a toy,
Amen, and then, Desus, I'll be a dood boy."

Their prayers being ended, they raised up their heads,
With hearts light and cheerful, again sought their beds.
They were lost soon in slumber, both peaceful and deep,
And with fairies in dreamland were roaming in sleep.

Eight, nine, and the little French clock had struck ten,
Ere the father had thought of his children again:
He seems now to hear Annie's half-suppressed sighs,
And to see the big tears stand in Willie's blue eyes.
"I was harsh with my darlings," he mentally said,
"And should not have sent them so early to bed;
But then I was troubled; my feelings found vent,
For bank stock today has gone down ten percent.
But of course they've forgotten their troubles ere this,
And that I denied them the thrice-asked-for kiss.

But just to make sure, I'll steal up to their door,
For I never spoke harsh to my darlings before."
So saying, he softly ascended the stairs,
And arrived at the door to hear both of their prayers;
His Annie's "Bless Papa" draws forth the big tears.
And Willie's grave promise fell sweet on his ears.
"Strange-strange-I'd forgotten," said he with a sigh,
"How I longed when a child to have Christmas draw nigh.
"I'll atone for my harshness," he inwardly said,
"By answering their prayers ere I sleep in my bed."
Then he turned to the stairs and softly went down,
Threw off velvet slippers and silk dressing-gown,
Donned hat, coat and boots, and was out in the street,
A millionaire facing the cold driving sleet!
Nor stopped he until he had bought everything
From a box full of candy to the tiny gold ring;
Indeed, he kept adding so much to his store,
That the various presents outnumbered a score.
Then homeward he turned. With his holiday load,
With Aunt Mary's help, in the nursery was stowed.
Miss dolly was seated beneath a pine tree,
By the side of a table spread out for her tea;
A workbox well fitted in the center was laid,
And on it the ring for which Annie had prayed,
A soldier in uniform stood by the sled
"With bright shining runners, and all painted red."
There were balls, dogs, and horses, books pleasing to see,
And birds of all colors were perched in the tree!
While Santa Claus, laughing, stood up in the top,
As if getting ready more presents to drop.
And as the fond father the picture surveyed,
He thought for his trouble he had amply been paid,
And he said to himself, as he brushed off a tear,
"I'm happier tonight than I've been for a year;
I've enjoyed more pure pleasure than ever before;
What care I if bank stock falls ten percent more!

Hereafter I'll make it a rule, I believe,
To have Santa Claus visit us each Christmas Eve."
So thinking, he gently extinguished the light,
And tripping down stairs, retired for the night.

As soon as the beams of the bright morning sun
Put the darkness to flight, and the stars one by one,
Four little blue eyes out of sleep opened wide,
And at the same moment the presents espied;
Then out of their beds they sprang with a bound,
And the very gifts prayed for were all of them found.
They laughed and they cried, in their innocent glee,
And shouted for papa to come quick and see
What presents old Santa Claus brought in the night
(Just the things that they wanted) and left before light:
"And now," added Annie, in a voice soft and low,
"You'll believe there's a 'Santa Claus,' papa, I know;"
While dear little Willie climbed up on his knee,
Determined no secret between them should be,
And told in soft whispers how Annie had said
That their dear blessed mamma, so long ago dead,
Used to kneel down and pray by the side of her chair,
And that God up in heaven had answered her prayer.
"Den we dot up and prayed dust as well as we tould,
And Dod answered our prayers; now wasn't He dood?"
"I should say that He was, if He sent you all these,
And knew just what presents my children would please.
("Well, well, let him think so, the dear little elf,
'Twould be cruel to tell him I did it myself.")

Blind father! Who caused your stern heart to relent,
And the hasty words spoken, so soon to repent?
'Twas Lord Jesus who bade you steal softly upstairs,
And made you His agent to answer their prayers.

Sophia P. Snow

Let the Lower Lights Be Burning

Brightly beams our Father's mercy,
From His light-house evermore,
But to us He gives the keeping,
Of the lights along the shore.

Dark the night of sin has settled,
Loud the angry billows roar;
Eager eyes are watching, longing,
For the lights along the shore.

Trim your feeble lamp, my brother:
Some pour sailor tempest-tost,
Trying now to make the harbor,
In the darkness may be lost.

Let the lower lights be burning!
Send a gleam across the wave!
Some poor fainting, struggling seaman,
You may rescue, you may save.

GOD

unto whom all hearts are open,
unto whom all wills do speak,
from whom no secret thing is hidden,
I beseech thee
so to cleanse the purpose of my heart
with the unutterable gift of thy grace
that I may perfectly love thee,
and worthily praise thee.

***

Doxology

Praise God from whom all blessings flow,
Praise Him all creatures here below,
Praise Him above ye Heavenly Host,
Praise Father, Son, and Holy Ghost.

***

Thank you Lord for all things bright and good. The
spring time, the harvest, our life, our health, our food.
No gifts have we to offer thee, for all that thou imparts,
but that which thou desireth, a thankful, humble heart.

***

Serenity Prayer

God, grant me the serenity to accept the things I cannot
change. Courage to change the things I can and the
wisdom to know the difference.

A treasure more precious than silver,
A treasure more precious than gold.
To find this hidden treasure,
You must look within your soul.

The Hidden Treasure Myth
"The Pearl of Great Worth"

George Rapanos

A HIDDEN TREASURE

Prologue

There is a virgin spirit that dwells in the soul of all mankind. Only in love will this spirit make its presence known, and only with the awareness of this spirit will the presence of God become visible in the form of a radiant light. This love is not the love of man for God, but the love of God for all mankind.

Life is more than an adventure

Once beyond time there was a Prince seeking a Spiritual Kingdom. He wandered into a forest vast and dark and became lost. While searching to find his way out, he thought he heard soft and compelling music. He listened intently as he followed the enchanting melody further and further into the forest.

He came upon a magically lit clearing where he saw a fairy princess playing a sweet melody on her golden flute. Her radiant beauty and the sound of her music went to his soul. Her entire being glowed with an angelic grace which manifested itself through her music. She was the princess of his dreams. At this very moment, the forest flashed with mystical light and the Prince became frightened and instinctively drew his sword. When the fairy princess saw him do this, she vanished, and so did the sound of her music.

The beauty of the princess and the melody of her flute haunted the Prince wherever he went. A spell had been cast upon him and he had no choice but to seek that which had frightened him and had also brought him so much joy. Being separated from that moment caused him pain and suffering.

He thought of her constantly. He had never seen her before and did not know where she had come from, or where she had gone. He searched every part of the forest around his earthly kingdom, yet he searched in vain. The memory of his experience filled him with both fear and hope. Although she had disappeared, her presence was always with him. Was it a dream? He cried out, "God, may this be reality and not a dream; but if it is a dream, let me dream on!"

He could not think of anything but that moment which had given him so much love and happiness. From that very moment the Prince became aware of what gave life its true meaning. He knew that he must continue his quest.

His journey brought him to a wise old sage who was reputed to have guided many men to their ultimate destinies. The Prince was told that what he was seeking was not a dream but could only be found in the dark recesses of an enchanted castle built by a vain and unhappy Queen seeking her own glorification.

She had built this castle so strong that it would be very difficult for anyone to penetrate it. The walls were covered with a million mirrors. This unhappy Queen needed these mirrors to give her or anyone who looked upon them the illusion of life, wholeness and security, but the cold, empty rooms only reflected her own emptiness. The sense of security that she had hoped for echoed fear instead.

The sage told the Prince that the Queen's daughter lived in this vast, deserted castle and was the beautiful, mysterious princess whom he sought. She was kept a prisoner in this castle by a spell her mother had cast on her when she was a little girl. The Princess was told that she "should not," and "ought not," leave the castle; this spell and the mirrors made her unable to find her way out.

The sage said that it was written in the stars that her spirit comes out at night and plays a soft, sweet melody with the hopes that someday, someone will hear her call <u>and come to be rescued.</u>

The sage also told the Prince that what is sought is in the very nature of the seeker, that happiness is not something to be gained, for it is already contained in oneself.

It had also been written that a gallant prince would come and, if his love and resolve were strong enough and he pursued her with a pure heart and with sincere intent, he would eventually penetrate these walls and find the love he was seeking. The Prince and the Princess would be able to live forever in the enchanted forest with eternal love in the Spirit and Kingdom of God.

The sage told the Prince how to find the castle and warned him that the road was long and difficult to follow. Although the wise man described many dangers, he also said, "If one's heart is pure and true to his dream, he will find and win whatever he is seeking."

After his long and arduous journey, the Prince finally reached the dark and forbidding castle. He knocked on the door and no one answered. He shouted for someone to let him in and, again, no one answered. He was frightened because he did not know what perils awaited him on the other side of the door.

His heart was captive and his soul was afraid, and he considered turning back. To overcome his fear, he gathered his courage and lifted the latch. The mighty door swung open.

Fear and terror seized him. His mind told him to run, that his search was in vain, but his heart told him to enter. The desire to succeed in his quest was greater than his fear. Such was his necessity that his courage cast away his fear and he entered.

Although he was frightened, the memory of the melody of the flute and the beauty of the princess pulled him into the unknown recesses of the castle. He drew his sword and lit a candle. Suddenly, he was faced with a million men, all with drawn swords and lighted candles. The reflection of the candles in the mirrors created a brilliant light and in the terror of that moment he knew what he had to do. In order to continue his quest for the Princess, he must do battle with each and every one of the warriors he saw.

He became frightened and standing before him were one million frightened warriors, ready for battle. He became aggressive and the warriors became aggressive. He raised his sword against these overwhelming odds and charged. As he struck at his foes, he heard the sound of breaking glass.

He then pulled back and to his surprise, his million adversaries pulled back. In a gesture of humility, he surrendered his sword. At the same moment, the million warriors who faced him also surrendered their weapons.

Bewildered by what had happened, he picked up a piece of glass that lay at his feet. Upon looking at it, he saw a warrior and realized that it was none other than himself, and that all the pieces of glass were only parts of a mirror. He looked deep into the mirrors and became aware that he was all alone, and that what he feared most was himself.

At that very moment, the obstacle which was himself, the barrier between him and what he sought, melted away. His face was illuminated by the brilliance and radiance of an ideal love, more beautiful than anyone can comprehend.

In this enlightened state, he saw himself as one is seen by those who love him. Because of his love for the fairy princess, he was absorbed in this love. All earthly possessions lost their value in this love. He came to the realization that where there is love, fear does not exist. All the warriors he had feared had now disappeared. What he had perceived was an illusion.

He came to a Self-realization of a forgotten and hidden truth, that God is within us all, but that, in order to find God, one must peel away all the illusions of the separate-self that are created by the ego, abandon the cravings and desires of this world and seek the hidden treasure—the perfect love that will cast away the fear of death.

One must recognize that nothing worthwhile can be done without the presence of God. Man would not so frantically pursue happiness unless, somewhere within him, there remained a glimmer of past bliss.

With this realization the Prince was able to leave the dark, sinister castle with a new-found freedom. From that moment he realized that whosoever will be free must die to the mortal desires of the ego and live in the life and spirit of God, a bliss within reach of all mankind.

As he walked from the castle, a sudden gust of wind blew out the candle and the castle walls crumbled into ruins. To his surprise and bewilderment, he was still bathed in a brilliant light from an unutterable source of existence. As he turned, he saw again the radiantly beautiful princess playing her golden flute.

He approached her with the love of God for all mankind. He felt that the Self-same Power that brought him to her also brought her to him, and their souls were united in the spirit of Love. At that moment he realized that he and the Princess were one. He said, "Here I am, the goal of life. Hear I am, all life!" This is the only reality that has ever existed, or that will ever exist.

A feeling of wholeness, peace, oneness and timelessness came over him, and he remembered the words and wisdom of Omar Khayyam:

Ah, my beloved.
Come fill this cup,
That clears today,
Of past regrets
And future fears.

There is no life until you have loved and been loved, for love transcends both fear and regret and exists wholly in the moment. Life is a free ongoing essence of 'Becoming," and a free ongoing essence of "Being." It is the immortality of the spirit of man.

Epilogue

One must have a spiritual initiation that comes by grace in order to begin the Quest for the essence of God. Those who are attached to the phenomenal world will give excuses for not making the effort needed for the journey. The awakened soul, guided by God's grace, will choose to make the journey toward complete fulfillment which is beyond the material world and leads to total affinity with God.

Life is Being

At the end of the Quest, the enlightened person will become aware that what he sought was none other than his true Self. He will know that the beings of creation and the Creator are indivisible; and that the essence of God has always been with him, guiding him from within, moment by moment, throughout his entire journey through life, if he would but listen.

THE HIDDEN TREASURE
"The Pearl of Great Worth"

There is a hidden Treasure,
Most search for it in vain.
It comes down from heaven,
And it falls like the rain.

This treasure is not one of silver,
This treasure is not one of gold.
The source of this hidden treasure,
Lies deep within one's soul.

A treasure more precious than silver,
A treasure more precious than gold.
To find this hidden treasure,
You must look within your soul.

Prologue
To Life Eternal

One should not be obsessed with a passing love. One should be in love with the Beloved, and the beloved is God. A rose is just a rose, but in its transcendental form it is the image and shadow of God.

It is not possible to truly experience God, the Hidden Treasure, by way of a passing love, until you stop mistaking the object of your desire for the treasure. The treasure is that which is found deep within your soul. The object of your love only leads you to the inner depths of your being, where you become aware of God's love and His existence.

Wisdom Tales

The Chinese Pilot

In the town of Surat, in India, was a coffee-house where many travelers and foreigners from all parts of the world met and conversed.

One day a learned Persian theologian visited this coffee-house. He was a man who had spent his life studying the nature of the Deity, and reading and writing books upon the subject. He had thought, read, and written so much about God, that eventually he lost his wits, became quite confused, and ceased even to believe in the existence of a God. The Shah, hearing of this, had banished him from Persia.

After having argued all his life about the First Cause, this unfortunate theologian had ended by quite perplexing himself, and instead of understanding that he had lost his own reason, he began to think that there was no higher Reason controlling the universe.

This man had an African slave who followed him everywhere. When the theologian entered the coffee-house, the slave remained outside near the door, sitting on a stone in the glare of the sun, and driving away the flies that buzzed around him. The Persian having settled down on a divan in the coffee-house, ordered himself a cup of opium. When he had drunk it and the opium had begun to quicken the workings of his brain, he addressed his slave through the open door:

"Tell me, wretched slave," said he "do you think there is a God, or not?"

"Of course there is," said the slave, and immediately drew from under his girdle a small idol of wood.

"There," said he, "that is the God who has guarded me from the day of my birth. Every one in our country worships the fetish tree, from the wood of which this God was made."

This conversation between the theologian and his slave was listened to with surprise by the other guests in the coffee-house. They were astonished at the master's question, and yet more so at the slave's reply.

One of them, a Brahmin, on hearing the words spoken by the slave, turned to him and said:

"Miserable fool! Is it possible you believe that God can be carried under a man's girdle? There is one God—Brahma, and he is greater than the whole world, for he created it. Brahma is the One, the mighty God, and in His honor are built the temples on the Ganges' banks, where his true priests, the Brahmins, worship him. They know the true God, and none but they. A thousand score of years have passed, and yet through revolution after revolution these priests have held their sway, because Brahma, the one true God, has protected them."

So spoke the Brahmin, thinking to convince every one; but a Jewish broker who was present replied to him, and said:

"No! the temple of the true God is not in India. Neither does God protect the Brahmin caste. The true God is Abraham, Isaac, and Jacob. None does He protect but His chosen people, the Israelites. From the commencement of the world, our nation has been beloved of Him, and ours alone. If we are now scattered over the whole earth, it is but to try us; for God has promised that He will one day gather His people together in Jerusalem. Then, with the Temple of Jerusalem—the wonder of the ancient world—restored to its splendor, shall Israel be established a ruler over all nations."

So spoke the Jew, and burst into tears. He wished to say more, but an Italian missionary who was there interrupted him.

"What you are saying is untrue," said he to the Jew. "You attribute injustice to God. He cannot love your nation above the rest. Nay rather, even if it be true that of old He favored the Israelites, it is now nineteen hundred years since they angered Him, and caused Him to destroy the nation and scatter them over the earth, so that their faith makes no converts and has died out except here and there. God shows preference to no nation, but calls all who wish to be saved to the bosom of the Catholic Church of Rome, the one outside whose borders no salvation can be found."

So spoke the Italian. But a Protestant minister, who happened to be present, growing pale, turned to the Catholic missionary and explained:

"How can you say that salvation belongs to your religion? Those only will be saved, who serve God according to the Gospel, in spirit and in truth as bidden by the word of Christ."

Then a Turk, an office-holder in the custom house at Surat, who was sitting in the coffee-house smoking a pipe, turned with an air of superiority to both the Christians.

"Your belief in your Roman religion is vain," said he. "It was superseded twelve hundred years ago by the true faith; that of Mohammed! You cannot but observe how the true Mohammedan faith continues to spread both in Europe and Asia, and even in the enlightened country of China. You say yourselves that God has rejected the Jews; and as proof you quote the fact that the Jews are humiliated and their faith does not spread. Confess then the truth of Mohammedanism, for it is triumphant and spreads far and wide. None will be saved but the followers of Mohammed, God's latest prophet; and of them, only the followers of Omar, and not of Ali, for the latter are false to the faith."

To this a Persian theologian, who was of the sect of Ali, wished to reply; but by this time a great dispute had arisen among all the strangers of different faiths and creeds present. There were Abyssinian Christians, Llamas from Tibet, Ismailians and Fire-worshippers. They all argued about the nature of God, and how He should be worshipped. Each of them asserted that in his country alone was the true God known and rightly worshipped.

Every one argued and shouted, except a Chinaman, a student of Confucius, who sat quietly in one corner of the coffee-house, not joining in the dispute. He sat there drinking tea and listening to what the others said, but did not speak himself.

The Turk noticed him sitting there, and appealed to him, saying:

"You can confirm what I say, my good Chinaman. You hold your peace, but if you spoke I know you would uphold my opinion. Traders from your country, who come to me for assistance, tell me that though many religions have been introduced into China, you Chinese consider Mohammedanism the best of all, and adopt it willingly. Confirm, then, my words, and tell us your opinion of the true God and of His prophet."

"Yes, yes," said the rest, turning to the Chinaman, "let us hear what you think on the subject."

The Chinaman, the student of Confucius, closed his eyes, and thought awhile. Then he opened them again, and drawing his hands out of the wide sleeves of his garment, and folding them on his breast, he spoke as follows, in a calm and quiet voice.

Sirs, it seems to me that it is chiefly pride that prevents men agreeing with one another on matters of faith. If you care to listen to me, I will tell you a story which will explain this by an example.

I came here from China on an English steamer which had been round the world. We stopped for fresh water, and landed on the east coast of the island of Sumatra. It was mid-day, and some of us, having landed, sat in the shade of some coconut palms by the seashore, not far from a native village. We were a party of men of different nationalities.

As we sat there, a blind man approached us. We learnt afterwards that he had gone blind from gazing too long and to persistently at the sun, trying to find out what it is, in order to seize its light.

He strove a long time to accomplish this, constantly looking at the sun; but the only result was that his eyes were injured by its brightness, and he became blind.

Then he said to himself:

"The light of the sun is not a liquid for if it were a liquid it would be possible to pour it from one vessel into another, and it would be moved, like water, by the wind. Neither is it fire for if it were fire, water would extinguish it. Neither is light a spirit, for it is seen by the eye; nor is it matter for it cannot be moved. Therefore, as the light of the sun is neither liquid, nor fire, nor spirit, nor matter, it is—nothing!"

So he argued, and, as a result of always looking at the sun and always thinking about it, he lost both his sight and his reason. And when he went quite blind, he became fully convinced that the sun did not exist.

With this blind man came a slave, who after placing his master in the shade of a coconut tree, picked up a coconut from the ground, and began making it into a night light. He twisted a wick from the fiber of the coconut; squeezed the oil from the nut into the shell, and soaked the wick in it.

As the slave sat doing this, the blind man sighed and said to him:

"Well, slave, was I not right when I told you there is no sun? Yet people say there is a sun.....But if so, what is it?"

"I do not know what the sun is," said the slave. "That is no business of mine. But I know what light is. Here, I have made a night light, by the help of which I can serve you and find anything I want in the hut."

And the slave picked up the coconut shell, saying: "This is my sun."

A lame man with crutches, who was sitting near by, heard these words and laughed:

"You have evidently been blind all your life," said he to the blind man, "not to know what the sun is. I will tell you what it is. The sun is a ball of fire, which rises every morning out of the sea and goes down again among the mountains of our island each evening. We have all seen this, and if you had had your eyesight you too would have seen it."

A fisherman, who had been listening to the conversation, said:

"It is plain enough that you have never seen beyond your own island. If you were not lame, and if you had been out as I have in a fishing boat, you would know that the sun does not set among the mountains of our island, but as it rises from the ocean every morning so it sets again in the sea every night. What I am telling you is true, for I see every day with my own eyes."

Then an Indian who was of our party interrupted him by saying:

"I am astonished that a reasonable man should talk such nonsense. How can a ball of fire possibly descend into the water and not be extinguished? The sun is not a ball of fire at all, it is the Deity named Deva, who rides forever in a chariot round the golden mountain, Meru. Sometimes the evil serpents Ragu and Ketu attack Deva and swallow him, and then the earth is dark. But our priests pray that the Deity may be released, and then he is set free. Only such ignorant men as you, who have never been beyond their own island, can imagine that the sun shines for their country alone."

Then the master of an Egyptian vessel, who was present, spoke in his turn.

"No," said he, "you also are wrong. The sun is not a Deity, and does not move only round India and its golden mountain. I have sailed much on the Black Sea, and along the coasts of Arabia, and have been to Madagascar and to the Philippines. The sun lights the whole earth, and not India alone. It does not circle round one mountain but rises far in the east, beyond the Isles of Japan, and sets far, far away in the west, beyond the islands of England. That is why the Japanese call their country 'Nippon' that is 'the birth of the sun.' I know this well for I have myself seen much, and sailed to the very ends of the sea."

He would have gone on, but an English sailor from our ship interrupted him.

"There is no country," he said, "where people know so much about the sun's movements as in England. The sun, as every one in England knows, rises nowhere and sets nowhere. It is always moving round the earth. We can be sure of this for we have just been round the world ourselves, and nowhere knocked up against the sun. Wherever we went, the sun showed itself in the morning and hid itself at night, just as it does here."

And the Englishman took a stick and, drawing circles on the sand, tried to explain how the sun moves in the heavens and goes round the world. But he was unable to explain it clearly, and pointing to the ship's pilot said:

"This man knows more about it than I do. He can explain it properly."

The pilot, who was an intelligent man, had listened in silence to the talk till he was asked to speak. Now every one turned to him, and he said:

"You are all misleading one another, and are yourselves deceived. The sun does not go round the earth, but the earth goes round the sun, revolving as it goes, and turning towards the sun in the course of each twenty-four hours, not only Japan, and the Philippines, and Sumatra where we now are, but Africa, and Europe, and America and many lands besides. The sun does not shine for some one mountain or for some one island, or for some one sea, nor even for one earth alone, but for other planets as well as our heart. If you would only look up at the heavens, instead of at the ground beneath your own feet, you might all understand this, and would then no longer suppose that the sun shines for you or for your country alone."

Thus spoke the wise pilot, who had voyaged much about the world, and had gazed much upon the heavens above.

"So on matters of faith," continued the Chinaman, the student of Confucius, "it is pride that causes error and discord among men. As with the sun, so it is with God. Each man wants to have a special God of his own, or at least a special God for his native land. Each nation wishes to confine in its own temples Him whom the world cannot contain.

"Can any temple compare with that which God Himself has built to unite all men in one faith and one religion?

"All human temples are built on the model of this temple, which is God's own world. Every temple has its fonts, its vaulted roof, its lamps, its pictures or sculptures, its inscriptions, its books of law, its offerings, its altars and its priests. But in what temple is there such a font as the ocean; such a vault as that of the heavens; such lamps as the sun, moon, and stars; or any figures to be compared with living, loving mutually-helpful men? Where are there any records of God's goodness so easy to understand as the blessings which God has strewn abroad for man's happiness? Where is there any book of the law so clear to each man as that written in his heart? What sacrifices equal the self-denials which loving men and women make for one another? And what altar can be compared with the heart of a good man, on which God Himself accepts the sacrifice?

"The higher a man's conception of God, the better will he know Him. And the better he knows God, the nearer will he draw to Him."

Leo Tolstoi

Footprints

One night a man had a dream. He dreamed he was walking along the beach with the LORD.

When the last scene of his life flashed before him, he looked back at the footprints in the sand. He noticed that many times along the path of his life there was only one set of footprints. He also noticed that it happened at the very lowest and saddest times in his life.

This really bothered him and he questioned the LORD about it. "LORD, you said that once I decided to follow you, you'd walk with me all the way. But I have noticed that during the most troublesome times in my life, there is only one set of footprints. I don't understand why when I needed you most you would leave me."

The LORD replied, "My precious, precious child, I love you and I would never leave you. During your times of trial and suffering, when you see only one set of footprints, it was then that I carried you."

Author Unknown

I AM with you always. Even until the end of the earth.

The Value of a Gem

A young man came to the Master and said that all Christians were wrong and many other things besides.

The Master removed his ring from his finger and handed it to him and said, "Take this ring to the market place and see what you can get for it."

No one among the market people offered more than a piece of silver for the ring.

The young man brought the ring back.

"Now," said the Master, "Take the ring to the jeweler and see what he will pay you for it."

The jeweler offered a thousand gold pieces for the gem.

The youth was amazed.

"Now," said the Master, "Your knowledge of Christianity is as great as the knowledge the merchant has of jewelry. If you wish to value gems, become a jeweler. If you wish to value Christianity, become a Christian.

Unconditional Love

There was a saint that had a promiscuous wife who was forever entertaining the lustful men of the village. All her suitors would judge, insult and ridicule him for her transgressions.

They would say, "How can you love your wife when she abuses you so?" and he replied, "I will answer that question with a question. 'How can God love anyone such as you?'"

The Gates to Heaven and Hell

A famous soldier came to the Master and asked, "Master, tell me! Is there really a heaven and a hell?" "Who are you?" asked the Master. "I am a samurai warrior of the great emperor's personal guard," replied the soldier. "Nonsense!" said the Master. "What kind of emperor would have you as his guard? To me, you look like a beggar!" At this, the soldier started to rattle his big sword in anger. "Oho!" said the Master. "So you have a sword! I'll wager it is much too dull to cut off my head!" At this, the soldier could not hold himself back. He drew his sword and threatened the Master, who said, "Now you know half the answer! You are opening the gates to Hell!" At these words the samurai soldier, perceiving the master's teachings, drew back and sheathed his sword and bowed. "Please forgive me," he said. "Now you know the other half of the answer," said the Master, "You now have opened the gates to heaven."

The Best of Two Potatoes

A youth came to the Master with hopes that the Master would enlighten him in spiritual awareness. The Master said, "Take these two potatoes and go outside and eat both of them. When you finish, come back and I will tell you if I will be able to help you or not but it is very important that you eat both of the potatoes."

He went outside and while he was eating the first potato, a begger came up to him and asked him if he could have the other potato because he hadn't eaten for days and was very hungry.

The youth gave the begger the other potato and the begger thanked him and went on his way. After eating his potato he went back to the Master. The Master asked him if he had eaten both of the potatoes as he had instructed him. The boy told him that he hadn't and that he had given the other potato to a hungry begger.

The Master then told the youth that he would not be able to help him and that there was nothing that he could do for him. Upon hearing this the boy went away.

Many years passed and the Master's friend asked him, "What ever happened to that young boy that you gave the two potatoes to eat?" The Master said, "The boy grew up healthy, strong and prosperous. He married well and had many healthy and happy children that all married well."

His friend said, "Didn't he have any bad luck?" And the Master said, "No. That was the other potato."

Publishing the Three Sutras

A Zen master decided to publish the sutras, which at that time were available only in Chinese. The books were to be printed with wood blocks in an edition of seven thousand copies, a tremendous undertaking.

The Zen master began by traveling and collecting donations for this purpose. A few sympathizers would give him a hundred pieces of gold, but most of the time he received only small coins. He thanked each donor with equal gratitude. After ten years the Master had enough money to begin his task.

It happened that at the time the river overflowed. Famine followed. The Master took the funds he had collected for the books and spent them to save others from starvation. Then he began again his work of collecting.

Several years afterwards an epidemic spread over the country. The Master again gave away what he had collected, to help his people.

For a third time he started his work and after twenty years his wish was fulfilled. The mothers tell their children that the Master made three sets of sutras and that the first two invisible sets surpass even the last.

There Are Too Many Saviors On My Cross

There are too many saviors on my Cross, lending their blood, to flood out my ballot box with needs of their own. Who put you there? Who told you that was your place? You carry me secretly naked in your heart, and clothe me publicly in armour, crying, "God is on our side," yet I openly cry, "Who is on mine? Who? Tell me, who?" You who bury your sons and cripple your father whilst you buried my Father in crippling his Son?

The antiquated Saxon sword, rusty in its scabbard of time, now rises. You gave it cause in my name, bringing shame to the throned head that once bled for your salvation.

I hear your daily cries in the far off byways, and your mouths, pointing north and south, and my Calvary looms again, desperate in rebirth. Your earth is partitioned, but in contrition, it is the partition in your hearts that you must abolish.

You nightly watchers of Gethsemane, who sat through my nightly trial delivering me from evil, now deserted. I watch you share your silver. Your purse rich in hate, bleeds my veins of love.

There is no issue stronger than the tissue of love, no need as holy as the palm outstretched in the run of generosity, no monstrosity greater than the ache you inflict. Who gave you the right to increase your fold, and decrease the pastures of my flock? Who gave you the right? Who gave it to you; who, and in whose name, do you fight?

I am not in heaven, I am here; Hear me. I am in you; Feel me. I am of you; Be me. I am with you; See me. I am for you; Need me. I am all mankind. Only through kindness will you reach me.

What masked and bannered men can rock the Ark and navigate a course to their anointed kingdom come?

Who sailed their captain to waters that they troubled in my fount, seeking in the ignorant seas of prejudice?

There is no virgin willing to conceive in the heat of any bloody Sunday. You crippled children, lying in cries on Darey streets, pushing your innocence to the full flush face of Christian guns, battling the blame on each other. Do not grow tongues in your dying dumb wounds, speaking my name. I am not your prize in your death. You have exorcised me in your game of politics.

Go home to your knees, and worship me in any cloth, for I was never tailor-made. Who told you I was? Who gave you the right to think it? Take your beads in your crippled hands. Can you count my decades? Take my love in your crippled hearts. Can you count the loss? I am not orange, I am not green, I am a half ripe fruit needing both colors to grow into ripeness, and shame on you to have withered my orchard. I in my poverty, alone without trust, cry "Shame on you, and shame on you again and again, for converting me into a bullet, and shooting me into men's hearts."

The ageless legend of my trial grows old in the youth of your pulse, staggering shamelessly from barricade to grave, filing in the book of history my needless death one April. Let me in my betrayal, lie low in my grave, and you in your bitterness, lie low in yours, for our measurements grow strangely dissimilar.

Our Father, who art in Heaven, Solid! Be Thy Name.

Author Unknown

The Greatest Swordsmith

Okasaki Masamura was the greatest swordsmith of ancient Japan. Not only was he famed as a master of the art, but as a man of inspiring moral stature as well. So great was his intensity of spirit, it is said that when he forged a sword, something of his own nature would pass into it. His ablest disciple Muramasa was reputed to have exceeded him in the keenness of his blades, however. A samurai, wishing to ascertain the finer edge, placed a Muramasa sword in a flowing stream. Every fallen leaf that floated down and met the blade was cut in two. He did the same with the sword of Okasaki. To his surprise, the floating leaves avoided the blade.

A Pile of Manure

Someone handed a man a pile of manure and told him that it was gold. He was told that whenever his hunger got to the point that he was near death that he should take this gold (the pile of manure) to the bank and redeem it for money to buy food in order to save himself from starvation.

Being a trusting soul this man never questioned the validity of what he had in his possession and went about life with the belief that what he had would, in the event of a crisis, save his life.

This man always followed the dictates of others. He never questioned the actions of his society, culture, religion, parents and teachers or of those he considered his superiors.

This man believed that what he had in his possession would give him security. What he really had was a false sense of security.

When this man's life was coming to an end and he was in desperate need of food, he took the pile of manure that he believed was gold to the bank for salvation and was told that it was worthless!

So it came to pass that this man, not having experienced for himself the true God, died from the lack of this wisdom. For anyone who truly knows God may not die but have eternal life.

Serenity

As a Zen master was fanning himself, a monk came up and said: "The nature of the wind is constance. There is no place it does not reach. Why do you still use a fan?"

The master answered: "You only know the nature of the wind as constance. You do not know yet the meaning of it reaching every place."

The monk said: "What is the meaning of 'there is no place it does not reach'?"

The master only fanned himself. The monk bowed deeply.

A powerful king, ruler of many domains, was in a position of such magnificence that wise men were his mere employees. And yet one day he felt himself confused and called his sages to him.

He said: "I do not know the cause, but something impels me to seek a certain ring, one that will enable me to stabilize my state. I must have such a ring, and this ring must be one which, when I am unhappy it will make me joyful and at the same time, if I am happy and look upon it I must be made sad."

The wise men consulted one another, and threw themselves into deep contemplation. Finally they came to a decision as to the character of this ring which would suit their king.

The ring which they devised was one upon which was inscribed the legend:

THIS, TOO, WILL PASS

A Matter of Projection

A man was passing from one village to another. On his way he saw a Sufi Master sitting on the side of the road. He stopped and asked him what the people were like in the village that he was going to.

The Master asked him how were the people in the village that he was coming from. He related to the Master all the negative aspects of the village and its people.

The Master proceeded to tell him that the people in the village he was going to were no different from the ones in the village that he was coming from.

Another man was passing by coming from the same village and upon seeing the Master stopped and asked him what the people were like in the village that he was also going to.

The Master asked him the same question that he had asked the previous traveler. How were the people in the village that he had just come from? He related to the Master all the positive aspects of the village and its people.

The Master proceeded to tell him that the people in the village he was going to were no different from the ones in the village that he was coming from.

A good man will find that there is goodness in the world; an honest man will find that there is honesty in the world; and a man of principle will find principle and integrity in the minds of others.

The Source of Eternal Life

Mind of the average human being is like a ship in which the sailors have made a mutiny. They've locked the captain and the navigator down below in the cabin and everybody feels very free. All the sailors feel the sense of complete freedom. One sailor, one part of the mind, steers for awhile, loses interest, leaves the wheel, another sailor, another part of the mind, comes up and steers for awhile. The ship goes essentially in circles. Very inefficiently. You feel free but real freedom consists in quelling the mutiny, bringing the Captain and the navigator up from below to take command again so that one can choose a goal and consistently and wholeheartedly with one's whole Being steer towards it.

Fear

A mulla saw a cloud of dust off in the horizon, "What could that be?" he said, "Must be a storm coming." After giving it some thought, he said, "It can't be a storm, it must be horses. What are they doing out there?"

After some time had passed and he had given it more thought he became frightened. He came to the conclusion that the horses belonged to the army. Now he wondered why the army would be out there. "They must be coming to the village to draft men into their army," he said and now he became very frightened and started to run, thinking that they were coming to get him. He ran into a graveyard and saw an open grave and jumped in.

The village people who knew him saw how frightened he was and ran after him. When they came to the open grave they looked in. There was the mulla staring up at them. "Mulla what are you doing here?" they asked and he replied, "I am here because you are here."

Greed or Sorrow?

When the mulla heard that his uncle had died and left him a million dollars, he began to cry. "Why are you crying?" they asked, "You have just become a millionaire."

Just then he was told that his other uncle had died and left him many more millions. Now he began to cry with even greater sorrow. "Why are you crying?" they asked. "You are now a very wealthy man," and he replied, "I am crying because I no longer have any uncles."

The Miser and the Angel of Death

A miser had accumulated, by effort, trade and lending, considerable wealth. He had lands and buildings, and all kinds of wealth.

He decided that he would spend a year in enjoyment, living comfortably, and then decide as to what his future should be.

But, almost as soon as he had stopped amassing money, the Angel of Death appeared before him, to take his life away.

The miser tried, by every argument which he could muster, to dissuade the Angel, who seemed, however, adamant. Then the man said: "Grant me but three more days, and I will give you one-third of my possessions."

The Angel refused, and pulled again at the miser's life, tugging to take it away.

Then the man said: "If you will only allow me two more days on earth, I will give you two-thirds of my wealth."

But the Angel would not listen to him. And the Angel even refused to give the man a solitary extra day for all his possessions.

Then the miser said: "Please, then, give me just time enough to write one little thing down."

This time the Angel allowed him this single concession, and the man wrote, with his own blood:

"Man make use of your life. I could buy not one hour for three hundred thousand dollars. Make sure that you realize the value of your time."

Unity

A little girl was crying because she had lost her doll. "If you stop crying I will buy you a new doll," said the father. "I don't want a new doll," cried the little girl, "I want my doll."

What the father did not realize was that his little girl had love invested in her doll and through this love, the little girl and the doll became one.

"I and the Father are one," said Jesus.

An Unutterable Source of Existence
Infinitely Higher Than Deity.

The King invited the most important people in his Kingdom to a banquet to be held in his honor. When a little old man arrived dressed in rags, he was taken to the King who upon seeing him shouted, "Who are you and what do you want? You look like a beggar."

The old man took this with historical good grace and replied, "You invited me." "Not so!" cried the King, "I only invited the most important people in my Kingdom."

"I am important," said the old man. "Are you a mayor?" asked the King. "Much higher," replied the old man. "Are you a governor?" "Higher still," answered the old man. To this the King shouted, "Who do you think you are, God?"

"Higher still," answered the old man. "There is no one higher than God," cried the King. "That's me," answered the old man.

The Juggler of Notre Dame

In the days when the world was young, there lived in France a man of no importance. Everyone said he was a man of no importance, and he firmly believed this himself. For he was just a poor traveling juggler, who could not read or write, who went about from town to town following the little country fairs, and performing his tricks for a few pennies a day. His name was Barnaby.

When the weather was beautiful, and people were strolling about the streets, this juggler would find a clear space in the Village Square, spread a strip of old carpet out on the cobblestones, and on it he would perform his tricks for children and grown-ups alike. Now Barnaby, although he knew he was a man of no importance, was an amazing juggler.

First he would only balance a tin plate on the tip of his nose. But when the crowd had collected, he would stand on his hands and juggle six copper balls in the air at the same time, catching them with his feet. And sometimes, when he would juggle twelve sharp knives in the air, the villagers would be so delighted that a rain of pennies would fall on his strip of carpet. And when his day's work was over, and he was wearily resting his aching muscles, Barnaby would collect the pennies in his hat, kneel down reverently and thank God for the gift.

Always the people would laugh at his simplicity and everyone would agree that Barnaby would never amount to anything. But all this is about the happy days in Barnaby's life. The springtime days when people were willing to toss a penny to a poor juggler. When winter came, Barnaby had to wrap his juggling equipment in the carpet, and trudge along the roads begging a night's lodging in farmers' barns, or entertaining the servants of some rich nobleman to earn a meal. And Barnaby never thought of complaining— he knew that the winter and the rains were as necessary as the spring sunshine, and he accepted his lot; "For how," Barnaby would say to himself as he trudged along, "could such an ignorant fellow as myself hope for anything better."

And one year in France there was a terrible winter. It began to rain in October and there was hardly a blue sky to be seen by the end of November. And on an evening in early December at the end of a dreary, wet day, as Barnaby trudged along a country road, sad and bent, carrying under his arm the golden balls and knives wrapped up in his old carpet, he met a Monk. Riding a fine white mule, dressed in warm clothes, well-fed and comfortable, the Monk smiled at the sight of Barnaby and called to him: "It's going to be cold before morning....how would you like to spend the night at the monastery?"

And that night Barnaby found himself seated at the great candle-lit dining hall of the Monastery. Although he sat at the bottom of the long table, together with the servants and beggars, Barnaby thought he had never seen such a wonderful place in his life. The shining faces of fifty Monks relaxing after this day of work and prayer.

Barnaby did not dare to suggest that he should perform his tricks as they would be sacrilege before such men, but as he ate and drank more than he had ever had at a meal for years, a great resolution came over him. Although it made him tremble at his own boldness, as the meal ended, Barnaby suddenly arose, ran around the table down to where the Lordly Abbot sat at the head, and sank to his knees: "Father....grant my prayer! I cannot hope to become one of you, I am too ignorant....but let me work in the kitchen and the fields, and worship with you in the Chapel!"

The Monk who had met Barnaby on the road turned to the Abbot: "This is a good man, simple and pure of heart." So the Abbot nodded, and Barnaby that night put his juggling equipment under a cot in his own cubicle, and decided that never again would he go back to his old profession.

And in the days that followed, everyone smiled at the eager way he scrubbed the floors and labored throughout the buildings; and everyone smiled at his simplicity. As for Barnaby his face shone with happiness from morning until night.

Until two weeks before Christmas....then Barnaby's joy suddenly turned to misery. For around him he saw every man preparing a wonderful gift to place in the Chapel on Christmas. Brother Maurice, who had the art of illuminating copies of the Bible. And Brother Marbode was completing a marvelous statue of Christ; Brother Ambrose, who wrote music, and had completed scoring a great hymn to be played on the organ during Christmas services.

All about Barnaby, those educated, trained artists followed their work....each one of them readying a beautiful gift to dedicate to God on Christmas day. And what about Barnaby? He could do nothing. "I am but a rough man, unskilled in the arts, and I can write no book, offer no painting or statue or poem....alas....I have no talent, I have no gift worthy of the day!"

So Barnaby sank deep into sadness and despair. Christmas day came....and the chapel was resplendent with the gifts of the Brothers....the giant organ rang with the new music; the choir sang the Chorales; the candles glittered around the great new statue. And Barnaby was not there....he was in his tiny cubicle, praying forgiveness for having no gift to offer.

Then a strange thing happened. On the evening of Christmas day, when the Chapel should have been deserted, one of the Monks came running white-faced and panting with exertion into the private office of the Abbot. He threw open the door without knocking, seized the Abbot by the arms. "Father....a frightful thing is happening....the most terrible sacrilege ever to take place is going on right in our own chapel! Come!"

Together the two portly men ran down the corridors, burst through a door, and came out on the balcony at the rear of the chapel. The Monk pointed down toward the altar. The Abbot looked, turned ashen in color. "He is mad!"

For down below, in front of the altar, was Barnaby. He had spread out his strip of carpet, and kneeling reverently upon it, was actually juggling in the air twelve golden balls! He was giving his old performance....and giving it beautifully....his bright knives....the shining balls, the tin plate balanced on the tip of his nose. And on his face was a look of adoration and joy.

"We must seize him at one," cried the Abbot, and turned for the door. But at that moment a light filled the church....a brilliant beam of light coming directly from the altar, and....both the Monks sank to their knees.

For as Barnaby knelt exhausted on his carpet, they saw the Statue of the Virgin Mary move; she came down from her pedestal, and coming to where Barnaby knelt, she took the blue hem of her robe and touched it to his forehead, gently drying the perspiration that glistened there. Then the light dimmed. And up in the choir-balcony the Monk looked at his superior: "God accepted the only gift he had to make."

And the Abbot slowly nodded: "Blessed are the simple in heart....for they shall see God."

Anatole France

Is That So?

The Zen master Hakuin was praised by his neighbors as one living a pure life.

A beautiful Japanese girl whose parents owned a food store lived near him. Suddenly, without any warning, her parents discovered she was with child.

This made her parents angry. She would not confess who the man was, but after much harassment at last named Hakuin.

In great anger the parents went to the master. "Is that so?" was all he would say.

After the child was born it was brought to Hakuin. By this time he had lost his reputation, which did not trouble him, but he took very good care of the child. He obtained milk from his neighbors and everything else the little one needed.

A year later the girl-mother could stand it no longer. She told her parents the truth, that the real father of the child was a young man who worked in the fishmarket.

The mother and father of the girl at once went to Hakuin to ask his forgiveness, to apologize at length and to get the child back again.

Hakuin was willing. In yielding the child, all he said was: "Is that so?"

Reality

A certain king in India, who was of a very realistic and logical mind, went to Shankara to receive instructions as to the nature of the Absolute. When Shankara taught him to regard all of his kingly wealth and power as no more than mere phenomenal illusions arising out of the absolute Self which is the ground of all things, the king was incredulous. And when he was told that the one and only Self appeared multiple only because of the dualisms of his ignorance, the king straight-away decided to put Shankara to a test and determine if the sage really felt this existence was no different from a dream.

The following day, as Shankara was approaching the palace to deliver his next lecture to the king, a huge and heat-maddened elephant was deliberately turned loose and aimed in Shankara's direction. As soon as the sage saw the elephant charging, he turned and fled in an apparently very cowardly fashion, and as the animal nearly reached him, he disappeared from sight. When the king found him, he was perched at the top of a lofty palm tree, which he had ascended with remarkable dexterity. The elephant was caught and caged, and the famous Shankara, perspiration pouring off him, came before his student.

The king naturally apologized for such an unfortunate and nearly fatal accident. Then, with a smile breaking across his face, but pretending great seriousness, he asked why the venerable sage had resorted to physical flight, since surely he was aware that the elephant was of a purely illusory character.

Shankara replied, "Indeed, in highest truth, the elephant is non-real and illusory. Nevertheless, you and I are as non-real as that elephant. Only your ignorance, clouding the truth with this spectacle of non-real phenomenality, made you Highness see illusory me go up a non-real tree."

Conditioning

To his surprise, the husband saw his wife cut a piece from a leg of ham and place both the cut piece and the remaining leg of ham in a pan to be cooked for dinner. He asked her why she had cut the piece off. She replied that it was because her mother did it that way.

He went to the mother and asked her if she cut a piece off a roast and then placed both pieces of meat in the pan before roasting them. She said that she did, because her mother had done it that way before her.

He went to the old women and asked if she also prepared meat by cutting off a piece and placing both pieces in the pan. She said that she did and explained that there was a time when her family was very poor and couldn't afford to buy a larger pan so she had to cut off a piece in order to fit the roast in the pan.

The Gardener

A stranger upon seeing a beautiful and bountiful garden went up to the gardener and said, "God and you have sure done a great job in cultivating this garden." To which the gardner replied, "You should have seen it awhile back, when God had it all by himself."

Freedom

Agamemnon wanted to become a god. He struggled for perfection but in the end he was overcome and defeated by Apollo who then placed an earthly curse on him and all his descendents.

The curse was that he and all his descendents would suffer because of man's craving and desirous nature.

Agamemnon had a son named Orestes and the son was in a serious dilemma because his mother Clytemnestra had killed his father. Should Orestes avenge the death of his father as Greek society demands?

Although nothing could be more evil in Greek society than matricide, the killing of one's mother. What should he do? He finally gave in to the demands of others and killed his mother.

From that point on the gods inflicted suffering upon him that was unbearable. He suffered mentally and physically for the wrong that he had done. After suffering for many years, he prayed to Apollo and said, "Haven't I suffered enough?"

Apollo contemplated the circumstances and said that he would grant him a trial in which all the Gods would be present. When all the Gods were assembled, Orestes pleaded his case and said, "Haven't I suffered enough?"

Apollo interceded in behalf of Orestes and said that Orestes' father wanted to become a god. In that struggle Agamemnon did battle with Apollo and was defeated.

Upon defeating Agamemnon, Apollo placed an earthly curse upon him and all his descendents. Orestes, being a descendent of Agamemnon, inherited that curse.

He related how he engineered it so that Orestes' mother would kill his father and that Orestes would then have to kill his mother.

Apollo pleaded with the gods that Orestes was not responsible for his actions because it was he alone that created the conditions that brought about the death of his mother.

Orestes quickly spoke up and said, "No, that's not what I'm saying. All I'm saying is, Haven't I suffered enough?"

Upon hearing this the Gods were astonished. Orestes wasn't blaming Apollo and the other Gods for his crime of matricide or even blaming his parents for their actions but was taking responsibility for his own actions.

From that day forward the Gods lifted the curse from Orestes and he was free. Orestes's nature now is one in harmony with that of the Gods.

Ye shall know the truth
And the Truth shall set you free.

Awareness

Two sages were standing on the bridge over a stream. One said to the other, "I wish I were a fish, they are so happy!" The second replied, "How do you know whether fish are happy or not? You're not a fish." The first said, "But you're not me, so how do you know whether I know how fish feel?"

I Want Your Finger

A poor man one day met an old friend who had become an immortal. After hearing his friend complain of his poverty, the immortal pointed his finger at a brick by the roadside, which immediately turned into a gold ingot. He presented it to his friend. When the man was not satisfied with this he gave him a big gold lion. But the man was still not appeased. "What more do you want?" asked his immortal friend. "I want your finger!" was the reply.

Weasel and the Well

The sun was beating down on Shulamis like an oven as she traveled through a desert of rocks and hills. She was lost, tired and thirsty. She fell without any strength next to a rock in her pathway. She called to God, "God, please have mercy on me and send help to this desolate place. Let my eyes be opened that I may see a well of water to drink from, so I may not die of thirst. Let me be good in Your eyes, and have mercy on me, as You had on Ishmael, the son of Hagar, whom You gave a Spring of water in the desert. He drank and his spirit lived."

Shulamis got up from praying on her knees. She looked behind her and saw a well of water next to one of the rocks. Her eyes lit up, she strengthened herself, ran to the place and called out in happiness, "God's name should be blessed, for He has not forsaken me. Happy is the person who has trust in Him."

She went to the well, and she saw there was a rope attached to it. She took the rope and pulled it, and behold there was no pail on the end. Shulamis observed the water in the well it was pure and crystal clear.

Because her thirst was so great, she took hold of the rope and went down into the bottom of the well and drank. Her spirit returned. She gathered her strength, grabbed the rope, and as she began to climb, the rope broke. Shulamis was left alone and frightened at the bottom of the well. She raised her voice, cried and pleaded to God for his mercy. "Your kindness to me was great. You opened my eyes to see a well of water in the desert. I drank and my eyes lit up and I was filled. Will You still have pity on me, and not let me die in this place and the well be my grave? Please God, have mercy on me and bring me out of this well and I will tell of Your righteousness to many.

At that time a young man was traveling by who had also strayed from the way. He sat next to one of the mountains to rest from the burden of his trip and shade himself from the heat of the sun which was burning like fire. He brought out bread, raisins and figs from his bag and ate. He said to himself, "I will rest a little and feast my heart so that I will have the strength to go further."

When he finished eating, he took out his flask to drink, and found that it was empty. He gathered his strength and traveled on until he came upon a well next to one of the rocks.

Shulamis heard his footsteps as he approached the well and called out to him, "Please save me!" The young men heard her calling for help and said, "Who is calling out to me?"

Shulamis answered, "Please listen to my pleas and save me from this well and I will do whatever you ask."

He threw Shulamis a rope, strengthened himself and said, "Hold onto the rope and I will pull you up."

Shulamis did as he told her and held onto the rope with all her strength and the man lifted her up and out of the well.

"Now that you have saved me from death, what is it that I may do for you?" asked Shulamis.

Seeing that she was very pretty, the man said, "Please become my wife and I will be good to you, for now God has granted me everything."

Shulamis approving of him said, "Yes, I will marry you. Blessed are you for the kindness you have shown me and saved me from death."

The young man said, "Promise me that you will be my wife."

Shulamis swore that she would and said, "Tell me your name." The young man answered, "I am

Aushalom." Shulamis said, "You must also promise me that you will not take another wife," and the young man made that promise.

It was at this moment that a weasel passed in front of the well. And Aushalom said, "The weasel and the well will be our witnesses, for we have both sworn to this oath." Shulamis answered, saying, "They are our witnesses."

Aushalom went on one of the highest mountains and there saw shepherds leading their sheep and ran after them. They showed him the paths that went to his and Shulamis' village. He quickly returned to Shulamis, who stood by the well waiting for him.

Aushalom took Shulamis and returned her to her father's house and left for his home in Jerusalem, promising to return so they could be married.

When Aushalom reached home he quickly forgot Shulamis and the promise he made to her.

Aushalom saw among the girls of Jerusalem, Avigail, who was pretty and wise. She found favor in his eyes from all the girls and he chose her for his wife.

After a period of time, Avigail gave birth to a son. Aushalom was very happy and gave a feast in honor of the occasion.

The guests were eating when suddenly a scream was heard coming from the room where the boy and his nursemaid were sitting.

Aushalom and all the guests were frightened. They quickly ran towards the scream. They came to the room and saw the boy lying on the floor, dead. The maidservant was holding her hands, crying and tearing at her hair.

They asked the maidservant what happened. She answered, saying, "I went out of the room to call my mistress and when I returned, I saw a weasel choking the child. I raised my voice and the weasel quickly jumped off the child and disappeared."

The happiness that Aushalom and his wife experienced that day ended and all the guests returned to their homes and Aushalom and his wife mourned the loss of their son for many days.

Time passed and Avigail gave birth to another son. Aushalom said to her, "Do not give him in the hands of a nursemaid but raise and protect him yourself so no misfortune shall come to him."

Avigail did as Aushalom said. She embraced her son and did not take her eyes off of him.

One day Avigail took her son to the garden. She passed by the well and heard the sound of birds chirping. She held her son tightly and as she bent her head to look into the well, her child tore himself away from her arms and fell into the well.

Avigail screamed a loud bitter scream. Aushalom heard her and ran to her side. He asked her with fear, "Where is the child?" In desperation she answered, "The child fell into the well."

The terror in the voices of Aushalom and his wife were heard in the courtyard. The servants and maids ran to the garden to see what happened. A servant went down into the well and brought out the child and it was dead.

Aushalom and Avigail mourned and cried until they had no more strength or tears to cry. Their relatives came to comfort and speak to them, but they could not be comforted, for their tragedy was very great.

When the days of mourning passed, Avigail said to her husband, "If our two sons would have died as people usually do, I would be at peace now, but I see that their manner of death is different from other people, for our children did not die from sickness or plague, but a weasel and a well killed them. I say that this is not a coincidence, but the providence of God. We should now look into our deeds and see where our sins were, because this is how God has punished us."

When Aushalom heard the words of Avigail he remembered his promise that he made to Shulamis. For the weasel and the well were the witnesses to his oath and commitment. In his desperation he called out, "I am the cause for the death of our sons!"

Avigail heard the words of her husband and became very frightened. She said, "Tell me what you did."

Aushalom told her all that happened to him in the desert and the commitment he made and did not keep.

Avigail listened and said, "God is righteous in all His ways! You profaned your holy promise and God inflicted your sin on our sons. Now, give me a divorce and I will return to my father's house and reflect and cry over the bitterness of my plight. You should go and honor you commitment to Shulamis. Take her as your wife and the anger of God will be lifted from you."

Aushalom listened to his wife and gave her a divorce. Avigail returned to her father's house and Aushalom went to honor his commitment and take Shulamis for his wife.

When Aushalom came before the hills of Shulamis' home, he sat by the shepherds to rest. The sun had already gone down, and it was night.

Aushalom asked the shepherds, "Do you know Manoack from Bais Lechen?" The shepherd answered, "And who doesn't know Manoach and the great tragedy which befell him? Ask a child from Bais Lechem, and he will tell you."

Aushalom became very frightened and said, "Will you not tell me what happened?"

The shepherd answered, "The wrath of God was poured onto him and his daughter Shulamis became insane." Aushalom became very startled and said, "And what is her insanity?"

The shepherd answered, saying, "It has been several years that his only daughter has been insane. And the words 'weasel and well' never leave her lips. Many doctors have tried to cure her but were unable to." The elder shepherd continued to speak to Aushalom and said, "It is very sad for us to see the suffering of Manoach and his only daughter. From the day his daughter became insane he has been very depressed and left the care of his sheep to us. When her father speaks to her, and asks her, 'What is it that ails you, daughter?' She doesn't answer, but cries. Her lips are moving and her eyes are looking up to the sky."

When Aushalom heard these words, he turned his face away from the shepherds and cried.

When morning came, Aushalom awoke the shepherds and one of them took him to Bais Lechem.

Aushalom came to the house of Manoach, and saw him coming out of his house. Aushalom said, "I have heard that you have a daughter and she is a good and fine woman. Will you let her be my wife so we may find peace in our houses?"

Manoach said, "God has made my daughter sick and the doctors are unable to cure her." Manoach told Aushalom about his daughter's sickness. Aushalom answered, "Let me come to the house and speak with her."

Manoach sighed with bitterness and said, "Your efforts will be all in vain! For you will hear her speak of nothing but the weasel and the well."

Aushalom came to Manoach's house and saw Shulamis, and he recognized her. He started to speak to her, and all she said was, "A weasel and a well!"

Aushalom said, "Remember the man who promised to take you for his wife, and the well which he took you out of, and the weasel which passed in front of it."

Shulamis got up and observed him. She cried out in happiness and said, "Are you Aushalom? Have you come to fulfill your promise?" In her joy she could not finish speaking for her eyes were filled with tears of happiness and she cried.

Aushalom said, "I have broken my trust with you and God has punished me. I have come today to ask your forgiveness and to fulfill my commitment which I spoke on that day."

Manoach saw his daughter speaking intelligently and he bowed down to God. He got up, and came close to Aushalom, and said, "You have cured my daughter. You have returned her to her senses which were stolen from her. Therefore, she will be your wife, and you will live and multiply and God will bless you."

Aushalom took Shulamis for his wife, and brought her to Jerusalem. God blessed them, for Shulamis gave birth to sons and daughters. They lived long lives, prospered and were a blessing in the midst of Israel.

You may ask, "What about the suffering of all the others in the story?" Now, that is another story.

God! Why hast thou forsaken me?
Why hast thou forsaken Me?

The rains came and the water overflowed the banks of the river so that George was prevented from seeking safety from the rising waters. So he prayed to God for help and God said, "Put your faith in me and I will provide."

The flood waters came up to the porch. Some men came by in a boat, and seeing George stranded on the porch, told him the waters were continuing to rise and asked him to get into their boat so they could take him to safety. George declined and said that he had put his faith in God and that God would provide.

It rained and it rained until the flood waters reached the roof of the porch and again the men in the boat came by and told him to get in so he could be taken to safety, for the waters were continuing to rise. George again declined and said that he had faith in God and that God would provide.

It continued to rain and the waters reached to the ridge of the roof. George was now hanging on to the chimney for dear life when a helicopter came down and told him to get in for if he didn't, he was sure to drown. He said that God had spoken to him and told him that He would provide.

George drowned, of course, and went to heaven. He could not understand why God did not help him in his hour of need, so he went straight to God and asked him that very question. "I put my trust and faith in you to provide and you let me down." God said, "I did provide. I came for you three times, twice in a boat and once in a helicopter."

Rather than ask for help, one should ask for guidance.

Imitation

Baso used to sit cross-legged from morning till night in constant meditation. His master saw him and asked: "Why are you sitting cross-legged in meditation?" "I am trying to become a Buddha," he answered.

The master picked up a brick and began polishing it on a stone nearby. "What are you doing, Master?" asked Baso. "I am trying to turn this brick into a mirror," was the answer. "No amount of polishing will turn the brick into a mirror, sir."

"If so, no amount of sitting cross-legged will make you into a Buddha," retorted the master.

Death Speaks

There was a merchant in Bagdad who sent his servant to market to buy provisions and in a little while the servant came back, white and trembling, and said, "Master, just now when I was in the market-place I was jostled by a woman in the crowd and when I turned I saw it was Death that jostled me." She looked at me and made a threatening gesture; now, lend me your horse, and I will ride away from this city and avoid my fate. I will go to Samarra and there Death will not find me. The merchant lent him his horse, and the servant mounted it, and he dug his spurs in the flanks and as fast as the horse could gallop he went. Then the merchant went down to the market-place and he saw me standing in the crowd and he came to me and said, "Why did you make a threatening gesture to my servant when you saw him this morning?" "That was not a threatening gesture," I said, "it was only a start of surprise. I was astonished to see him in Bagdad, for I have an appointment with him tonight in Samarra."

W. Somerset Maugham

Cause and Effect

My teacher took me for a walk through the town one day. A man on a donkey would not make way for us in the narrow streets, and as we were slow in getting out of his path he cursed us roundly.

"May he be punished for that behavior," people called out of their doorways.

My teacher said to me, "How simple-minded people are! Little do they realize how things really happen. They only see one kind of cause and effect, while sometimes the effect, as they would call it, appears before the cause."

I was perplexed and asked him what he meant.

"Why," he said, "that man has already been punished for the behavior which he showed us just now.

"Last week he applied to enter the circle of the elite and was refused. Only when he realizes the reason will he be able to enter the circle of the elect. Until then he will continue to behave thus."

Calling Card

A great Zen teacher was the head of Tofuku, a cathedral in Kyoto. One day the governor of Kyoto called upon him for the first time.

His attendant presented the card of the governor, which read: Kitagaki, Governor of Kyoto.

"I have no business with such a fellow," said the Zen teacher to his attendant. "Tell him to get out of here."

The attendant carried the card back with apologies. "That was my error," said the governor, and with a pencil he scratched out the words Governor of Kyoto. "Ask your teacher again."

"Oh, is that Kitagaki?" exclaimed the teacher when he saw the card. "I want to see that fellow."

Does the End Justify the Means?

A boy prayed to God for a bicycle. He prayed and prayed for a bicycle. After a period of time the boy got tired of praying to God for a bicycle and went out and stole one.

He then prayed to God for forgiveness.

Salvation

We are like the beggar who has been begging all his life in the same place. He wanted to be rich, but he was poor. When he died they found a treasure of gold buried just under the place where he had been begging. If he had only known how easy it was to be rich. True knowledge of the Self is salvation.

The Angel of Death

The angel of death came to a lost soul one evening and said, "Its time for you to come with me." "I'm not ready," he said. "I have a lot of work yet to accomplish. I must do this and that and be here and there." "You still must come," said the angel of death.

"Take my son instead of me," said this lost and wretched soul. The angel of death was surprised by such a request and said, "You are not serious are you?" "Yes, I am," said the lost and wretched soul. "Take my son."

"I've never had a request such as this before," said the angel of death. He turned and asked the son, "Are you willing to go in your father's place?" and the son replied, "I love my father with all of my heart and I am willing to go in his place." The angel of death accepted the trade and left.

After another lifetime the angel of death came back and said, "It is now time to go." And this lost soul again said, "No! I'm not ready to go, I have so much more to do, you must take my other son." And again the angel of death was surprised and asked the son, "Would you like to go in your father's place?" The son said, "I love my father with all of my heart and soul and I will go in his place."

Another hundred years passed and another. Each time the angel of death came for this lost soul, and left with another one of his sons. After a thousand year passed, the angel of death came again to take another son and the father said, "No! this time you will not take any more of my sons. It is time for me to go."

This surprised the angel of death and he asked, "What has changed?" The enlightened soul with grace and love replied, "After all these years, I've seen my sons go in my place because of their love for me. I did not realize that they had found the meaning and purpose of life at such a young age. It has taken me a thousand years to become aware that love is the meaning and purpose of life. No matter how long I live, my work will never be finished and that nothing is more important than love."

Acceptance

"Everyone is made perfect by God!" shouted the preacher. "Everything in the world is perfect!" he shouted again.

After the sermon was over, a hunchback, stooped over, went up to the preacher and said, "If God made everything perfect, then Why!" pointing to his deformity, "am I a hunchback like this?"

The preacher looked at him and smiled with grace and said, "Why, you're the most perfect hunchback that I've ever seen."

Happiness consists in being willing to be what you are.

Ignorance

A man that had worked most of his life was retiring. His son asked him, "What are you planning to do for the rest of your life?" He replied, "I'm going to ask God for His forgiveness because I have ignored Him for so long."

Enlightenment

One Thousand men went to hear the Master speak of Truths with hopes that his message would enlighten their souls. When they all arrived the Master was not there. After a period of time three hundred and thirty-three of them said, "If the Master cannot discipline himself to be here on time, there is nothing that he can teach me?" And they left.

Time passed and still the Master hadn't come and another three hundred and thirty-three said, "If the Master is not concerned about our feelings, why should we wait any longer for him?" And they left.

It was dark now and the remaining three hundred and thirty-four waited patiently until the Master did arrive. He staggered into the hall, stumbled and fell. The Master was intoxicated.

Upon seeing this three hundred and thirty-three more said, "If he can't take care of himself, how then can he help us?" And they left.

There now was only one soul remaining to hear the Master speak and upon hearing his message he acquired with humility what he perceived with wisdom to be Truth and became enlightened.

Intuitive Perception

The Emperor Cho entered the temple to meet Joshu who was doing zazen in his room. The assistant monk announced him. Joshu said, "Let the Emperor come in and make his bows." The Emperor came in and made obeisance. Right and left they asked him, "The Emperor and many courtiers have come, why don't you stand up?" Joshu said, "You don't understand me. If it is a visitor of low standing, I go out to the gate to meet him. If he is of middle class, I come down from my seat. If he is of high class, I greet him from my seat. The Great Emperor cannot be treated as a person of low or middle rank; I dread to insult him in such a way." The Emperor was highly delighted and two or three times paid homage to him.

> A weak man is in need of power.
> A strong man has no need for power.

A Fable of Two Brothers

Long ago, in a village far away, there lived two brothers who were as different as two people could possibly be. In fact, you could search the whole world over and be unlikely to discover two young men with so little in common. For whereas the elder was studious, the younger cared nothing for books and learning; and while the elder was courteous, the younger tended to be quite rude; and though the elder ate and drank moderately, the younger ate gluttonously and drank like a proverbial fish.

The elder brother aspired to be a zaddik, a righteous one, and to that end he applied himself with unmitigated diligence. Early in life he had been called by a deep inner longing to live an austere and ascetic existence. He prayed and studied ancient wisdom. He resisted comfort and complacency and avoided, as much as was humanly possible, all earthly pleasures. All, that is, except one. The sole diversion he did allow himself, if it could be called that, was to sing each evening a single hymn of jubilation.

The positive example set by the elder brother was, needless to say, not for a moment emulated by the younger. Quite to the contrary, the only mandates which the younger brother was interested in fulfilling were those of his untamed urges. Indeed, it was with deliberation equal to that of his older brother's piety and goodness that the younger brother engaged in all manner of pleasure. His reckless, wasteful pursuits had made him a local legend, and truly his reputation was well deserved. "Eat, drink and be merry!" might well have been his motto, although, "Live for today for tomorrow we may die!" would have applied just as aptly. For he could eat any three men under the table, and was sometimes heard to threaten that he might one day drink the entire county dry—a threat which was not lightly taken. He was the life of any party and quite a lady's man, too. The younger brother was always accompanied by a close circle of promiscuous women and a cluster of friends.

For fear that the reader might credit the younger brother's popularity to wit, charisma, charm, or even to his vainly handsome appearance, it should be explained that such was anything but the case. Nor should the younger brother's renowned generosity be mistaken as an emblem of a compassionate heart. In truth, the state of affairs that existed then was no different than the one that endures to this day. It has never been terribly difficult to find those who would gladly assist one in squandering an inheritance, no matter how meager it might happen to be. And as for the younger brother's generosity, it was born not from kindness, but rather from guilt, so deeply ingrained that it was not even perceived by him, much less admitted to. Unlike the elder brother who had been a good and dutiful son, the younger brother had rarely lifted so much as a finger in his late father's behalf.

Lest the reader be inundated by mistaken impressions, it must also be clarified, before this humble parable advances one sentence further, that the notable contrast in their personalities caused the brothers to harbor no great animosity toward each other. Despite their differences, there was, in fact, hardly a morsel of hostility between them. Their upbringing by a kindly merchant, recently deceased, and a loving, doting mother instilled in them tolerance and a disposition to live and let live. They got on well, for the most part, though neither approved of the other's way of life. They had their share of arguments, though in the end when the heat of the battle cooled, all would be forgiven.

It came as no great surprise when the two brothers bid farewell to their separate circles of friends, gave their mother farewell kisses and numerous assurances of their safe return, and set out walking one sunny morning in the late spring of the year 1653 toward a distant mecca of art, commerce and culture. Their intended aims and expectations for making this journey, like the brothers themselves, were as different as night and day. The elder brother hoped to find a certain zaddik who was rumored to be seeking a spiritual apprentice. The younger brother, however, had heard tales of the city's many lewd and passionate pleasures, of which he hoped to sample all but a few.

The days passed amicably. Mile after mile, village after village, county after county, they walked, conversing and arguing good-naturedly, occasionally pausing to gaze upon some uncommon sight, to hear some unusual sound, or to rest and eat by the banks of an algae-laden pond or a fast-running brook. At night they went their separate ways. While the elder brother read the Torah by firelight, meditated, and sang his nightly hymn, the younger brother would either eat and drink himself into a stupor or would go off in search of women and song. He had no need to search for wine, for he always made sure he carried a generous supply with him.

On their journey the younger brother was attacked by a band of thieves who sprang from the bushes, beat him about the head and shoulders, and made off with his purse. Luckily, this was one rare instance when the young reckless and wasteful brother had the uncustomary foresight to give the better part of his money to his brother for safekeeping. All he suffered on that occasion was a minor financial loss, a slightly blackened eye, and a mild case of wounded pride. Luck was also with him on another evening when a jealous husband, with a lantern jaw and hammer fists, tripped on a cobblestone, thus allowing him the precious seconds he needed to make a clean escape.

A week passed, and the better part of another. The halfway point was well behind them. The elder brother felt thoroughly invigorated. Not so the younger brother whose constant drunkenness and nightly jaunts were taking a heavy toll. Mornings were most difficult for him. He detested rising until the sun's disagreeable glare had begun to wane in the evening sky. On the road, however, it was imperative for them to put in as many miles as possible during daylight hours.

Rather than admit to the adverse effects of his over-indulgence, the younger brother would always bravely rise at the elder's prodding, laugh off his aching head and pretend that all was well. Thus, he would stoically go forth with throbbing temples and squinty, dark-rimmed, bloodshot eyes, a dull ache in the pit of his stomach, and a sour aftertaste left over from the previous evening's revelry that often would linger through most of the day.

As might be expected, the younger brother soon tired of this imposing appearance and was greatly pleased and relieved when a fierce storm struck one evening at a time when they happened to be in sight of a rustic, though agreeable looking, village inn which would, he hoped, afford him a quiet room, a hot bath, and a chance to recuperate from the past night's adventures. His expectations, however, proved ill-founded. When the two brothers inquired as to the availability of lodgings, the innkeeper, though seemingly sympathetic, informed them that several other travelers before them had sought shelter from the storm, the result being that every room was taken. After seeing the younger brother's debilitated condition, the innkeeper did offer, for a modest sum, to set up two cots in a corner of the room that was used by the inn's patrons for eating and drinking alcoholic beverages.

While in no sense an ideal situation, the brothers considered the cold, wet alternative and accepted the innkeeper's offer—the elder brother thinking that perhaps fate had brought him here with the object of furthering his spiritual education; the younger brother having no thoughts other than to rest his aching head and weary bones. While he was reluctant to admit it, the younger brother was feeling more flushed, feverish, and utterly wretched with every passing minute and wanted nothing more than to sink into oblivion.

Ruddy, rowdy, rotund, figures crammed the smoke-drenched dining room. Townsfolk, farmers, peasants, and travelers were talking, smoking, drinking, laughing and all of them seemingly intent upon making as much noise as possible while consuming as much as was humanly possible. These were the younger brother's kind of people, and on any other night he would have joined the festivities, but on this particular evening the very sight of so much gusto was enough to cause his head to spin and his stomach to do lazy cartwheels in sympathy.

While the innkeeper and his wife were setting up two cots in a shaded corner of the room, three of the patrons, thick of hand and girth, called over to the brothers in drink-thickened voices, offering to buy them a drink. The brothers smiled politely, waved across the noisy smoke-filled room while patting their lumpy hay-filled mattresses as if to say, "Thanks but no thanks," and the three burly men resumed their drinking.

At the younger brother's request, the elder brother took the cot nearest the wall, while the younger brother occupied the one closest to the night's festivities. The younger brother's location was based on the possibility that his dizzy head and churning stomach might give him cause to bring about a hasty retreat out of the thick, unpainted, weathered-hardwood door. Thus they settled in as best they could, to sleep.

The elder brother had not the least difficulty getting to sleep. Minutes later, when the younger brother complained about the smoke and the noise, the elder brother, who was facing the wall, snoozed heavily in reply. For the younger brother's sleep was as illusive as a swarm of fruit flies. The noise, the smoke, the uproar and laughter seemed in his increasingly feverish condition to be conspiring against him. The laughter and clatter seemed to be mocking him, twisting his ears, prying open his sweat glands, stirring up the vat of vinegar soup in his stomach while drilling pin-size holes in the sides of his head to release the resulting fumes. The evening's revelry seemed to be going on right inside his skull, his nerve endings, and in the very marrow of his bones. At other times, the babel of voices no longer seemed human, but like the barking of a kennel full of rabid strays. He tossed and twisted, stirring restlessly for an hour or two, before those yelping hounds of hell dragged him, kicking and screaming, into a fitful though blessed insensibility.

About that time it dawned upon the three thick-set revelers, who had earlier asked the brothers to share a drink with them, that perhaps the two strangers had refused them not out of simple fatigue, as their motions had seemed to suggest. Instead, perhaps, one of them suggested, their refusal to drink with them might have been the result of just plain "high-and-mightiness." Perhaps, added another, in the coarsest imaginable language, they thought themselves too good to drink with three men who made their living by the sweat of their brows and the strength of their backs. In no time, the brothers' simple gesture of refusal, in the hazy brains of the three muscle-bound drunkards, had been blown all out of proportion, taking on the dimensions of a hard slap across the face. Worse, an insult to their manhood! More serious even than that, a curse on their grandmothers' graves! This was exactly the sort of effrontery that no self-respecting oaf could, in good conscience, take sitting down.

With this in mind, the three ruddy-faced drunkards arose laboriously from their overburdened chairs and wobbled over to have a closer look at the two insolent snobs who had the foolishness and rash boldness to judge good men based upon the sketchiest evidence. Whereupon they loudly cursed and belittled the manhood of those who would spurn them and then rudely sleep through such a glorious festival of over-indulgence as they had offered to share with these two sleeping ingrates.

Being that the younger brother's cot was positioned nearest them, it was he upon whom the brutes started beating. A hand must have instinctively leapt out as he was waking and struck one of his attackers quite forcibly on the cheek. At least that was one of the complaints lodged against him as they hauled him from his bed, still half asleep, and commenced to push him around and then to slap him and hit him with repeated blows to his body and his undefended face and head.

As for the possibility of freeing himself, there was none. As for reasoning with them, that too was impossible. His protests fell on deaf ears. As for why they were doing this, he had not the slightest idea. All he did know was that three vaguely familiar brutes with hot, stale breath, scowling red-veined faces, and anvils where their hands should have been, were beating him half senseless for no apparent reason. Worse, his fever and depleted condition gave him neither the strength nor the conviction to give back even half so good as he was getting. So there he was, hardly able to defend himself and without even the benefit of his customary instinct for self-preservation, which under normal circumstances was quite considerable.

Fortunately for the sake of our young casualty, the innkeeper intervened to mediate on his behalf before the brutes had inflicted upon him serious injury. This act of intervention was hastily nullified by other deeds which were, to the victim's way of thinking, an outright travesty of justice. Instead of having the louts arrested, as the owner of any respectable establishment would have done, or at the very least escorting the drunkards to a bum's rush into the cold night, the innkeeper coddled the thugs and called them all by name! Instead of a swift kick into the stormy night, he gently chided the drunken brawlers in a tone that carried no more indignity than one would use on an errant child who had purposefully spilled a glass of milk. Was this not an outrage? Here he was, simply ushering the ruffians back to their table, leaving the battered victim with nothing but an apology for what was euphemistically termed "an inconvenience!"

Contempt gave way to bitterness, pain to self-pity, as the younger brother sat on the lumpy mattress and nursed his wounds. He had a split lip, a lump on his head, possibly a cracked rib or worse, and his attackers were back at their seats ordering another round and being treated as if they had created no more than a minor annoyance. Where was the fairness in this world? Where was the justice?

And where had his brother been while all this was going on? Hard though it was to imagine, the man had been, and still was, deep in slumber! Dead to the world! Sleeping like a statue! Why does one not travel alone, he angrily wondered, if not for sake of having one's traveling companions there for protection? A wave of incoherence suddenly came crashing over the rocky shore of his inner being, causing him to conclude, unreasonably, that somehow his sleeping brother was to blame. Whereupon, he leaned over and roughly shook the elder brother.

The elder brother awoke to a barrage of harsh criticism for not having risen to his brother's defense. Seeing his brother's condition, he felt only sympathy for him and not the slightest contempt. Indeed, his compassion grew more emphatic with his relating of each passing affront and insult. The poor man had obviously reached his breaking point. Finally, with quiet words of comfort, he persuaded his younger brother to try to go back to sleep. The younger brother agreed to this suggestion in principle, but fearing a repeat performance by the brutes, asked that the elder switch beds with him. The elder brother more then gladly complied, as any loving brother would have done under similar circumstances.

Be not mistaken as to the nature of the motivations of those who aspire to become zaddikim. While it may be true that a zaddik does not shy away from life's hardships and uncertainties, and it is true that he denies bodily comfort, he does so not out of some masochistic yearning, but for the purpose of achieving the greater pleasure that can be derived by completing the soul's cycle of correction. Thus the elder brother welcomed the opportunity to place himself between the thugs and his irate brother. If his body did receive a beating, well so be it! Certainly it would be for a reason. Perhaps some wrong deed in the past demanded retribution. At all events, he would accept what fate or providence had in store, firm in the conviction that the pain suffered by his body would be serving a higher purpose, namely, the purification of his soul. And so it was that the two brothers traded places and eventually drifted off to sleep.

Sure enough, later in the evening, as fate would have it, or perhaps it was providence, it dawned upon one of the three thugs that they had attacked only one of the disrespectful strangers, while sparing the other. This, in his inebriated judgment, did not seem equitable. Both were guilty of the same holier-than-thou impudence. Both had demonstrated equal conceit by refusing to share a drink with them. In good conscience, they could not beat up on only one of the contemptuous newcomers and let the other off scot free. Justice demanded that the other receive equal retribution. The incident, long forgotten by the brothers but in the benumbed brains of the three brutes, had become a matter of honor, principle, and integrity. Fair, after all, was only fair.

The brutes rose from their seats and lumbered over to the shadowed corner in which the two brothers were sleeping, both of them facing the wall. The thugs had no idea that the two brothers had switched beds, so quite naturally it was the man who was sleeping in the bed closest to the wall who was the target of their animosity. Thinking that the man closest to them had already received his comeuppance, they took great pains not to disturb him. They dragged the younger brother out of bed a second time and gave him a thorough beating, while the elder slept like a newborn babe.

A strange sensation overcame the younger brother as his body was suffering that second attack. Attribute it to fever, a concussion, or merely the utter absurdity of the situation, but he hardly felt the blows that were hailing upon him from all sides and angles. Whatever the cause, he was suddenly catapulted into an exquisite state of awareness, higher, purer, more lucid by far than any he had previously imagined. In those moments of mystical recognition his life came into clear and perfect focus. The facade of illusion with which he had always protected himself began to crack and then to crumble, leaving him alone with the naked reality of his empty existence. He saw it all: the futility of his self-indulgence and pursuit of pleasure, the vulgarity of his coarse nature and the true agony of his moral decay.

Those few seconds of mystical revelation taught him more than a lifetime of self-indulgence. And to whom did he owe this transformation, if not the brutes? He laughed! How he laughed! Which, as it happened, did much toward lessening the severity of the beating. So uproarious did his laughter become that the oafs lost the thread of their concentration and became confused and disoriented. Little satisfaction can be derived, especially from one who takes pleasure in the beating!

The elder brother awoke to the sound of laughter, not just that of his brother but of others that had also been bitten by the contagious laughter, including the brutes themselves! At that moment, he too underwent something of a transformation, for he understood what had happened and immediately realized that indeed fate, or some power higher than themselves, had guided them to this inn on this rain-swept night.

The two brothers never did complete their journey to the city. They had no need to. In that one evening they had intuitively transcended any further need for restless wandering and the emotional agonies that pass for worldly experiences. And so it was that they returned to their village. The two brothers had become "zaddikim" or righteous ones. They lived long, productive, loving lives in the village and through the years many seekers traveled from far and wide to request their counsel or simply to pay respects.

In their later years, the two wise zaddikim would sometimes recall with fondness the night in the village inn, and remember the two beatings which the younger had suffered at the hands of those three brutes. And, as always, they would smile, bless the brutes, and thank them in their evening prayers.

"Praise the name of God. Praise the servants of God."

The Guarantor

A certain lucrative business proposition once presented itself to a person who had fallen on hard times, but it would require a considerable capital outlay. Since he was down to his last penny, he decided to approach the most prosperous man in town for an interest-free loan for the amount.

"But you are not exactly a man of means. If I lend you money, on whose guarantee am I to lay my trust?" asked the prosperous man. The borrower replied, "On the guarantee of Him in Whom all lay their trust."

Upon hearing this, the prosperous man said, "On His guarantee I am willing to rely without any hesitation," and lent him the entire sum.

The transaction was exceedingly profitable, and in due course the borrower came to return the loan. The man refused, saying, "I have already received the amount in full."

"When did you receive the amount?" shouted the borrower. "I have not yet repaid you a single penny!"

"True," said the lender. "But did I not agree, on your own suggestion, to lend you the money against the guarantee of Him in Whom all lay their trust? And already, I assure you, my Guarantor has repaid me the whole amount, with interest!"

> Seek ye first the Kingdom of God and all its righteousness; and all things shall be added unto you.
>
> Matthew 6:33

Said the Lord, "I am Alpha and Omega,
the beginning and the ending . . ."

"I will be with you always"

NOTES

1   Farid-un-Attar, <u>The Conference of the Birds.</u>

2   Samuel Taylor Coleridge, <u>The Rime of the Ancient Mariner.</u>

3   Edna St. Vincent Millay, <u>Renascence.</u>

4   Hosea 2:14

5   Dag Hammarskjold, <u>Markings.</u>

10   Joseph Parry

11   Fanny J. Crosby

12   John Newton

13   Author Unknown

14   George Rapanos